Why I Believe

Why I Believe

A Psychologist's Thoughts *on* Suffering, Miracles, Science, *and* Faith

DR. HENRY CLOUD

NASHVILLE NEW YORK

Worthy
Hachette Book Group
1290 Avenue of the Americas, New York, NY 10104
worthypublishing.com
@WorthyPub

First Edition: June 2024

Worthy is a division of Hachette Book Group, Inc. The Worthy name and logo are registered trademarks of Hachette Book Group, Inc.

Library of Congress Control Number: 2024932964

ISBNs: 9781546003410 (hardcover), 9781546003434 (ebook)

Printed in the United States of America

LSC-C

Printing 1, 2024

To all those who honestly seek

Contents

Preface 1

Introduction 5

Part I: How I Came to Believe in God

1 Small Spiritual Beginnings 13

2 Seek and You Will Find 27

3 The Phone Call 36

4 Into the Abyss, and out of Egypt 40

5 A Leap of Faith 59

Part II: How I Came to Believe in Miracles

The Naked Pastor 79

God as GPS 83

He Protects 85

God's Provision 89

Reunion with Jesus 96

God's Perfect Shrink for Me 104

My Biggest Miracle 111

Do Not Sign It 117

Kneecap 122

A Helping Hand 126

A Day-to-Day Life with Jesus 131

Part III: How I Came to Believe through Science

6 The Truth Is True 137

7 Dynamic Tension and the Mind of Faith . . . 145

8 Science as an Obstacle to Faith 152

9 Can I Trust the Bible? 166

10 Jesus, Please Explain Your Followers 180

11 The Greatest Obstacle of All 197

12 Psychology and Faith 223

Conclusion and an Invitation to You 251

Acknowledgments 258

Notes 262

Preface

I have an issue . . . and this book is my attempt to solve it.

I have had this issue since I was about ten years old . . . and although it is better, it is still unresolved in my heart with so many of you . . . my friends. I won't name you by name here, but maybe you will find yourself in these pages. And for those who read this book whom I don't know, if you fit the description of how I describe my friends, then come along for the ride. We would probably be friends anyway. But, enough about you for a moment . . . I want to talk about me and my problem.

Here it is in a nutshell: I love God, and I know beyond a shadow of a doubt that He is real. He has proven that to me for decades. That is not my problem.

My problem is that I love my friends, and many of them do not know God, at least in any way that they have told me about. So the problem is this: I want them to know Him and know that He is real. I want them to have a relationship with Him and know how incredible that is.

So why is that a problem? Simple . . . I often do not know how to tell them.

"Wait . . ." you might say. "You have told millions of people about God in talks and books and media, so how is it that you don't even know how to tell your own friends about Him?"

Here is the simple answer . . . the audiences sign up to hear what I think about God. My friends don't.

They sign up to just be my friend. And I love that. That is why I signed up with them as well. They rock . . . my friends are the coolest people in the world. They are smart, funny, talented . . . many of them do amazing things in some field of endeavor, in their families, or some other way. Others don't set any records at all . . . they are just normal folks, and awesome as people. But all of them have one thing in common: they have the greatest hearts. They are honest, caring, and real. I love hanging out with them. And for some strange reason, they like to hang out with me as well.

Which brings me to the point. When we do hang out together, they did not come to talk about God. They just came to be together . . . to play golf, have dinner, talk about life. And so, my problem is that I don't want to bug them or make them uncomfortable by telling them what I want them to know about God. And I especially don't want to make them feel so weird that they would not want to hang out anymore . . . thinking I am somehow trying to "convert them," as one of my good friends said one time. (We laugh about it now . . . but at a party one time, he told a group that when he met me twenty years ago, he googled me and all of this "faith" stuff came up along with my being an author and psychologist. He thought, "Oh no . . . He's *one of those*, and he's going to try to convert me.") But as he told that story to another friend at a party at my house recently, he said, "I finally figured out that he [meaning me] was sort of normal and wasn't trying to do that." He and I and the other people in the conversation just laughed.

That conversation was funny . . . and I would never want to put pressure on anyone, make them feel uneasy, or weird, or judged for their own beliefs. So, for those reasons I often have this problem: *Even though they do not want to feel weird, and I do not want to make them feel that way, I still want my friends to know that God is real, and I want them to meet Him.*

And I struggle with that.

But that is not being a good friend, either . . . a good friend *does* share what they think their friend would love to know and have if they knew, right? But I often don't. And what do I know? They even might *want* to know what I think about God.

So, I decided to solve my problem. I am writing down some of my thoughts about God . . . for my friends. The stuff we never talked about.

Introduction

One night, as a ten-year-old at camp in North Carolina, I felt a pain and stirring in my soul that has never gone away. The night had been a regular camp night . . . with counselors and cabin mates at the big bonfire . . . doing camp-like things. One of them I do remember being a bit unusual . . . we ate a rattlesnake that some crazy counselor had killed, but other than that, just normal stuff, along with some kind of "devotional" time. It was a "lightly" Christian camp, but not an in-your-face overbearing type of religious camp. Mainly it was a sports and wildlife experience for four weeks of fun and some attempt by the counselors at spiritual and character development of who knows what kinds of kids had been sent there by parents wanting either a break or a better version of their kid. My parents probably hoped for both. ☺

That week had been one of a difficult-to-explain heightening of my love for God. I had always had a strong consciousness of God from early childhood . . . I somehow knew He was there. He showed Himself to me in ways I can't really explain . . . I just knew when I felt His presence and that it was real. But this particular camp experience that week led me to a little mountainside chapel as I was out for a hike, where I had an experience that I remember as if it were yesterday. I was tromping around in the Blue Ridge Mountains of North Carolina and suddenly felt drawn into that little building. As I sat there in silence, I was overcome with a movement in my heart. I felt Him drawing me to Him . . . it was kind of overwhelming, in a good way. The love was so strong that I felt for Him. As I sat there, I told Him that I would do whatever He wanted me to do with my life. I had been moved by an Invisible Force that I knew was real and loving. I was sure of that.

Which brought me to that night . . . I had heard it before, the "gospel" message that was conveyed, that God loved all of us and Jesus had died to pay the penalty for everything we had ever done wrong, securing forgiveness for any of us for all time. I had believed it before as a child but probably didn't understand it as well as I did that night. For some reason, this time it pierced me more deeply.

I don't remember all of the details of the message, but I vividly remember the gist. The counselor said that the gospel was a simple message that was like this: Think of if you committed a crime, and went to court, and were found guilty by the judge. You are standing in front of the bench, and he pronounces the verdict: guilty as charged. And then he pronounces the penalty, the fine. You know that you cannot pay it or endure it, but it stands as true and real. You are guilty, and you are convicted. You must pay the fine. And you also realize that you cannot afford the price.

Then, right at that moment, the judge says, "I will come down from the bench and stand in your place and pay the fine for you if you want me to. You may go free if you want to accept my offer." The counselor then said, "That is what Jesus did for us. He paid our fine, and if we accept His payment, his death on the cross for us, we can go free and be pronounced 'not guilty.'" We can be forever forgiven by God for everything we have ever done, or ever will do. It has been paid for, if we accept it.

Somehow the simplicity of that moved me in a different way than it had ever before. I realized that the love that I had felt from

God was from a loving Father, not mad at me for being "bad," and not ready to zap me for any mistake. It came together in a much deeper way.

So, with all of that good news, why the pain that night?

I felt the pain of knowing that my best friend did not know God . . . did not know that there was Someone who loved him this much and that he could have a relationship with . . . and I wanted him to know it, too. But I felt squeamish about how to tell him. After all, we were much more concerned with being cool and tough and winning games and trophies than being one of those weird religious types. So, I had never talked to him about it. And that night, I cried with my counselor in front of the fireplace back at the lodge. I needed to know how to get out of this dilemma . . . the dilemma of carrying around such an incredible Reality that I knew he would want to know, and at the same time being too afraid to talk about it.

Well, since that time, a lot has happened. A lot. And I have seen way, way more of how real God is, and what He can do. And this book is my attempt to put my journey with God into words . . . for one purpose: I want my friends to know that God is real. And although I have discussed God with many of my friends since that time, I want to write it all down for them and others I have not talked to, in one place: "You might think I am crazy, but this is why I believe, and why I want you to have a relationship with Him, too." And before you read on, I can pretty much guarantee that you will find some of it to sound very crazy. But it is all true.

But there are a lot of obstacles to faith. I had them myself after I decided to get more serious about my faith later in life, so it is easy for me to understand when others have those questions. I had to struggle with finding answers that satisfied me, because I could not be a believer and put my brain in a lockbox in order to do that.

So, the first purpose of this book is to share with you my story of God's reality in my life, and the second is to share how those hard questions were resolved in my own soul and brain. I want to share the answers I found that put it all to rest.

Life has so many dilemmas that make it so hard to believe in a good God at times, and the people who sell the God message can sometimes be so weird and crazy and obnoxious that we just feel like "If this faith were true, then all of that crap would not exist that surrounds it, and Christians would not be so undesirable and such a turn-off." As I used to think when I was a kid, "I like God; I just don't like His friends."

Of course, not all Christians are "that kind." So, so many are awesome people who do truly incredible things. They give of their time, talents, and resources to make the world a much better place, alleviating poverty, suffering, and much more. And they are people of stellar character. I know this to be true over and over, all around the world. But as I talk to people who do not share my faith, the experiences that they have had with some believers are often a big part of the obstacle to God. But the fascinating thing I have found is this: the religious people that you and I both struggle with and can't stand are the same ones that Jesus didn't get along with, either. I will show you what He actually says about certain types of judgmental, narrow-minded, narcissistic, and controlling religious types. I will hopefully help you discover something I learned . . . that "they" are not what He or the faith is about at all, and those people often do exactly the opposite of what He told us to do, even doing those things "in His name."

More about that later.

So, come along with me as I share my experience, my questions, and the answers that I have found that have satisfied my doubts. One disclaimer: I do not mean that my answers are even the best ones out there; they are only my heartfelt attempt to tell my own story about how they got answered for me. They come from many areas of science, and other fields, and as I studied those disciplines, I discovered something. There are brilliant people on both sides of faith and non-faith, and it told me that intelligence, IQ, science, philosophy or any other discipline is not standing in the way of whether or not someone believes. But for someone who does believe, the science supports faith, and as I will share with you, many of the most brilliant physicists, biologists, astronomers, and others who attest to that.

So, let's hop in. First my journey to faith and its experiences, and then how some tough questions got answered.

Part I

How I Came to Believe in God

One

Small Spiritual Beginnings

I am not trying to write a memoir of my life . . . that would be much too boring and trivial for anyone to spend time reading. What I do want to do, however, is to write the story of my *spiritual life* in a way that you can walk through some of the key experiences and learnings with me . . . and understand where I am coming from when I think about God.

I grew up in Vicksburg, Mississippi, a small city on the Mississippi River. It was a great place to grow up, with all of the positives of a small town. Kind of a combination of what was a city, yet close to all things rural and country, at the base of the Mississippi Delta—one of the world's fertile places for both creativity and suffering. Great outdoors activities such as hunting, fishing, water-skiing, horseback riding, golf, and the like were a regular menu of life there, as well as all kinds of other sports. The town was a close community of families and friends. My parents owned and operated a small business there for over forty years, and I grew up in a family that was very engaged in that local community.

My parents introduced me to faith early in life, and they were active in a local Methodist church. They gave much of their time and service to the poor. They also taught me that life was always lived before God, but they did so in a pretty low-key traditional way of attending church on Sunday, and showing one's faith through service to others, and being good citizens. Sunday school from early on, and overall, trying to be a good neighbor was what faith looked like in our house. Not too intrusive, mind you, but quietly meaningful. A good Southern Methodist clan, they were. But I never got the feeling that we had a "religious" home . . . it was just a normal Southern home where faith was the guiding, but not oppressive or overbearing, background.

My mother would say bedtime prayers with me each night, in the tradition of "Now I lay me down to sleep." My father could be seen reading his Bible and attending church regularly, but we had nothing like family devotions or that kind of overt "faith" training. That was left to the Sunday school teachers. Faith wasn't spoken about as much as just lived and assumed.

My father was a very regular "guy's guy," a lot more fun than some of the more "religious" parents of my friends. A World War II first sergeant, Daddy was pretty tough, but he was also loving and really, really funny. He always brought laughter to the moment or situation. Yet you always knew that he stood for things; he had strong principles, and one of those was his faith. He was serious about it, just not very loud about it. And he had friends from all walks of life. I really loved that about him. He loved having barbecues with laborers as much as hanging out in boardrooms, probably even more.

So, in that way, I did grow up in a Christian family, just not in an over-the-top way.

Our home was a gathering place for people of all kinds. My parents were really good people, and everyone loved them. It was not unusual for them to be lauded for their work in the community. I looked up to them in those ways, and just assumed that everyone was like them. It was normal in our small town for people to serve others and take care of them.

They volunteered for Meals on Wheels. My dad was chairman of the board of the Salvation Army and used his business to be very involved in helping the Black community in various ways at a time of clear segregation in the Deep South. He was older when I was born and had grown up in the Great Depression . . . so he always had a heart for the poor and people who were disadvantaged in some way. He came from poverty, built a very good business, and always used his business to help support our community. He was dedicated to taking unskilled young men off the street, training them in the trades around construction, and building careers for them. Many of his employees worked for him for over thirty years. Many of them he had taken from illiteracy to reading blueprints and being foremen on construction jobs. It was a skill he learned in life and the Army . . . having been a poor kid on the streets himself, taken in by an organization and being trained by them, then doing the same for others. When he retired in his sixties, instead of selling the business or leaving it to my sisters and me, he gave the company and all of its equipment to his employees, many of whom he had taken from the streets and helped them build careers as I mentioned. Both of my parents worked in the business, and I always felt like they were as much social workers as they were business owners.

One story that shows how he lived out faith more than talked about it is my favorite. He was in his twenties when World War II started, and he had enlisted in the National Guard. They gave him an IQ test, and he scored in the genius level, even though he had dropped out of school to support his family in the eighth grade. His father had died, and they were very poor. But the lack of schooling had not destroyed his natural intelligence, so the Army began to train him in leadership. They moved him to be head of an intelligence group that built the models for General Patton and others to fight their campaigns in Europe.

The interesting thing about that group, though, is that his men were all artists, sculptors, and set designers from Hollywood . . . non-soldiers who had been recruited to build the models that the generals used to plan battles, generals like Patton. They built rooms of mountain ranges, cities, and other topography so that the strategies could be formed, since back then there was no computer modeling.

So my dad found himself in the first part of his tenure in Europe as a young sergeant turning moviemakers into soldiers. These young men he led were displaced in England, away from home, separated from their families, lonely, and often just feeling lost. They were in the real throes of war and, not being soldiers, probably feeling pretty scared in the midst of all the bombings and destruction in Europe. And my dad, who had been in the military since he was eighteen, had compassion for them. He was tough, sometimes even harsh, but he had a heart.

One night my father went into town and got into a craps game (as I said, he was Christian but not overly religious), and after a few early wins, got in with some heavy hitters. He kept playing, and won what amounted to a lot of money that night. So he devised a plan for what he was going to do with it.

As someone who loved to eat and was very sick of army food in England and who at the same time felt sorry for his young soldiers who were away from home and also without good food . . . he went out and secretly, under the radar, bought a restaurant the next week in Henley-on-Thames, the town where they were stationed. He paid in cash.

Since this was not permissible for him as a foreign service-man to own a business or property in England, he found an older couple to run the place and agree to act like they owned it while they operated it so no one would know it was his. This set him up to execute his secret plan.

Tea and other foods had been rationed in parts of England, and he had a lot of these provisions from the base that he could use it as barter with the farmers in the countryside. So, each week, he would drive into the country and trade tea to farmers for chickens and potatoes. Then, he would bring them back to the older couple and tell them to close the restaurant on Saturday night and throw a party for the US soldiers with fried chicken and french fries. It was all free, and they could bring their dates. Just a gift of appreciation from an old English couple to the American soldiers. And no one ever knew who was actually behind it all, my father the illegal restaurateur. And the kicker? When he left England to go to join the liberation of France, he gave the restaurant to the old couple as a gift to them for all they had done.

I had heard this story many times from him and his war buddies over my childhood, and later, when I graduated from college, he took me there and showed me the town, the yacht club where the Cambridge-Oxford regatta was held that had been their headquarters, and the restaurant itself. I will never forget it. I have a painting of the yacht club in my study.

This story exemplifies the way that faith was shown to me by my parents as a kid. It was real, present but lived out much more in giving and caring for others than being overtly religious. My mother was the same way. She was *always* doing for others . . . the elderly people who were shut ins could always depend on her dropping by to check on them. She had two widows whom she cared for until they died in their nineties. She was always making sure that I went to visit them at least once a week or more, just to check in and make sure they had some company. It was not a suggestion . . . it was a *requirement.*

She tutored poor children in reading, delivered meals, and kept the nursery and toddlers in the Sunday school hour of our church for twenty years. My mother was always doing something for people who were struggling. And there were countless other good deeds I saw my parents do over my entire childhood—real expressions of their goodness and faith—not efforts to seem religious.

This kind of faith was pretty normal in our small Southern town. Faith was pretty private and social, yet real. At our house, probably the most overt practice of spirituality other than being regular churchgoers was just saying grace before meals and my father's Tuesday morning men's breakfast club at the church, which he would take me to.

So, for much of my early life, my faith was pretty much like that too . . . private and silent, but still real to me. I always believed in God. Sunday school helped reinforce a lot of it . . . learning about God and a little bit of the Bible, and just accepting it all as true. Sunday school was way more social than theologically grounding, but at least it reminded us that we were all there because of God in some way that we probably never even fully understood.

The gift of this is that from early on, I just somehow knew God was there . . . I even felt Him at various times. He seemed pretty constant and close. Sometimes too close, I thought, in terms of how I would see Him when I was "bad." I remember specifically one time getting into trouble when I was pretty little and going into our basement telling Him, "God I know I am bad, but You made me. So you are the one Who made me bad . . . but I am the one getting in trouble for it. That's not fair." And it really didn't seem fair to me at all, but I just accepted it and would move on. Still, being "bad" and getting into trouble for various childhood misdemeanors, and trying to be "good" at the same time, not ever really knowing which side was winning.

I was always confused in that way, not sure if I were a "good boy" or a "bad" one. That had a lot to do with trying to be good and at the same time frequently dipping into forbidden waters. Such was the early life of faith. Later, when I became a psychologist, I learned that much of that guilt and judgment was coming from voices other than God . . . in some ways my mother . . . who could expertly use guilt and shame as a parenting tool, and in other ways my World War II first sergeant father whose tough correction could sometimes scare the crap out of me.

Suffice it to say that I had a strong God consciousness from early on, along with an unhealthy dose of confusion at times about our relationship. A lot of this also had to do with my friends and the people I preferred to be with. I identified much more with the "normal" gang than the "church" types. Even though I would not always do all the things some of them did, they were the ones I liked the most (later, I discovered that Jesus and I had that in common . . . He hung around the fun crowd, it seemed, more than the religious ones).

I talked to Him a lot . . . I saw Him in everything, especially the beauty of nature and creation. It always made sense to me that Someone made the beauty of the dark woods I hunted and rode horses in; of the lakes I swam, fished, and water-skied in; and of the smells of spring, especially the grass after a downpour. I was a golfer from early in life, and I will always have the smell of fresh green grass deep in my soul, especially after a rain. I knew God made that. And the thunderstorms. No doubt the scary thunder was His, and it probably kept me in line at times.

I spent a lot of time talking to Him when I was alone, and I had a lot of alone time. My mother worked in the family business, and many of my days as a kid were spent alone when I was not engaged in sports or play. In the woods, horseback riding, on my bike, hunting or fishing, or especially on the golf course. I spent a lot of time alone and with God, talking to Him about life. Some of my most spiritual times were as a kid, riding my horse alone through the woods, just talking to God.

I remember as a very small child, sitting alone in the yard, playing in the grass, or digging with my little shovel. Then, if a bird would fly by, or I would notice a car that would suddenly divert my attention away from what I had been doing, immediately I would be baffled by an early spiritual dilemma: free will versus external determinants. When the bird caught my glance, and I looked up at it, realizing that I was now focusing on something in a different direction that I had been looking before the bird diverted me . . . it left me with a quandary: if that bird had not flown by, I would not be looking here. I would be looking in a different direction altogether, and the rest of my day would have followed that direction and would have been different as a result. One action that I did not cause had started a chain of events that had the potential to alter my life forever.

And I would ask God, "Okay, if I had not seen that bird, or that car, I would still be looking at the shovel. And now I am doing something totally different, down a completely different path, looking at trees or the sky and no longer playing in the dirt. My course of life has changed because of that bird. *Am I in control of my life or not?* Did *You* cause that? Are *You* in control of my life, or me? Or the bird or the car? That wasn't *my* choice . . . it just happened, and now, here I am." This was a pretty daunting question that I recall often asking God to help me understand. Who controls what happens and where we end up? I guess I was getting prepared for being a psychologist, but the point is that those kinds of discussions with God were frequent. He was always in my awareness, and we were always in relationship. I just knew it was real. Not like I know now, as it had never been tested, but it just felt real from an early age.

Another spiritual question I always struggled with was the existence of time and my place in it. I would be sitting in the yard, noticing what I was doing in the "now," and then I could remember what I had done before, say, that morning. And then I could remember breakfast, and even yesterday. But before that, it would get fuzzy. Why couldn't I remember my whole life all the way back to the beginning if I could remember what occurred that morning? And how did this moment of "now" move into something as lost as my "past"? Why wasn't all of my life all present and available to be now? It would be many years later, studying neuroscience, NDEs, quantum physics, and relativity, when I understood just how complicated these questions were, but it was just another example of ongoing conversations with God. Somehow, I always thought He must have an answer for even my most complex questions, and I talked to him a lot about my early dilemmas.

These experiences—watching my parents live their lives in our community and hanging out with God as a companion and recipient of my many existential questions—represented the extent of my "spiritual life" as a child. As I grew older, I became aware of something that troubled me: there were two groups of people with whom my spiritual life did not align.

First, there were the hard-core church people, with whom I did not identify at all, and they were very different from my family. They seemed to have a *lot* of rules . . . like not being able to go to dances or movies, or play poker, or bet on rounds of golf. Or, for some, even playing golf on Sunday. Ouch! I always felt a bit bad around them and judged by them . . . and at the same time, felt like I was sort of like them, as we both believed in God. Kind of like I was in their club, sort of, and not, at the same time. I think I was like my dad . . . he loved God but kind of poked fun at some of the overly religious types. He used to say if the Baptists moved out of town, the liquor stores would all go broke. But . . . we were like them, too.

Second, there were the people who did not have anything to do with God that I could see, nor did their families. In some ways, I could relate to them, too, and in some ways, even more. They did all the activities that I loved and were much more chill. They would even go water-skiing on Sunday! But especially as I got older, these folks would also engage in other pursuits that I knew my parents wouldn't approve of and some of which I didn't either—although frequently, I might be present and along for the ride, so to speak. I loved being with them, listening to the Allman Brothers or Led Zeppelin, just not getting high like they were.

So as I grew older, I began to feel like I did not totally belong to either group. It seemed like I was not as "bad" as they were sometimes and not as "good" as the church crowd. "Lost in the middle" was how I would spiritually classify my personal denomination. That feeling continued for a long time . . . and remains in some ways still today.

The dilemma of being spiritual deep in my heart and at the same time not at being able to fully identify with "religion" or "church types" was the predominant theme of my early years. I wanted to talk to my best friend, who was a pretty wild kid, about God, and yet I feared he would see me as "one of them." I didn't know what to do with friends like him, and as I have told you, sometimes I still don't. I held on to my secret spiritual life, unable to be one of those religious types, and so I felt like I had no place to land, like a spiritual wanderer without a true home. So, it was pretty much just me and God. And that was pretty much the path of my spiritual life until college. I had a relationship with God and always felt like I was not as spiritual as I should have been.

But there was one overt "God event" in my early years that has become important to my understanding of my spiritual evolution and became some sort of anchor for me to know that God was in my life. One Sunday morning, when I was almost four years old, I was sitting on the floor at Sunday school when my left leg began to hurt badly. It got worse until my parents had to be called in. I remember they took me home, and there was a flurry of activity going on in the house as they were calling doctors, trying to figure out what to do. I vividly remember a very ominous dark feeling that day. I was outside sitting on the grass waiting for the doctors and decisions to be made, in pain, and I had a strong realization that life had changed somehow. It felt really dark.

I did not realize who true that was.

Later that day I was hospitalized, and the doctors began working to find out what was wrong with me. My parents would tell me later that I would scream in pain for many nights, and how frightened they were. I was in agony, and they felt helpless. The doctors did every test they knew to do, and I remained in the hospital for some time, around a month, I think. I vaguely remember people coming to visit, lots of blood tests, x-ray machines, doctors in white coats, people poking me, and a lot of fear surrounding that time. I remember nights in the hospital with sitters I didn't know at times and feeling very scared and alone. I think that was some of the toughest parts of it . . . feeling alone.

So, the God moment: at some point, the doctors were considering amputation of my leg, and my mother had taken me to the appointment with her best friend, Emmett, accompanying her. Emmett was like my second mother and the mother of my best young childhood friend, Ike. They were a second family to me, and she was walking through this whole crisis with us, as well as her husband, who was a local physician and chief of staff at the hospital where I was being treated. The doctor was late to the appointment, and we waited there for him for a long time. As we waited, my mother heard a voice, saying, "Leave here, and take him to Oschner in New Orleans." Oschner was the big training hospital of the South, sort of like the Mayo Clinic or Cleveland Clinic of the South at that time. It was the place you went when all else failed.

Mama turned to Emmett and said, "Come on. We are leaving." I am sure that Emmett was confused, but my mother was certain because of the Voice she had clearly heard. She took me home and somehow convinced my otherwise levelheaded father to obey a voice telling them to drive 225 miles with no doctor, no plan, no referral . . . just a direction straight "from God."

They took me to Oschner and checked me in, and I was "randomly" assigned to a new orthopedic surgeon named Dr. Mary Sherman. It turned out that this assignment was not so random.

I went in to see her and vividly remember her examining me, sending me for X-rays, and calling me and my parents back in. She seemed larger than life to me . . . very outgoing, very pretty, so confident, and so kind. She looked at them and said, "There will be no amputation. I know exactly what this is and how to treat it." She went on to explain the disease in my hip and the treatment protocol that would ensue. I would be in a wheelchair for a while, then on leg braces and crutches for a longer time, up to two years. And then, "He will be fine."

Amazingly, Dr. Sherman had moved to New Orleans from Chicago, where she had been trained specifically in the newest treatment of this disorder by the ones who had developed it, and she was one of the most heralded international bone specialists in the entire world at the time. As it turns out, there was no one anywhere who would have been better. As my parents understood and always told me, the voice my mother had heard was God leading them and answering their prayers to help them know what to do when they had no options. Hitting the end of the road, hearing a voice, standing up to the experts they were trusting, getting specific instructions to go to a specific hospital, and a "random" assignment to one of many possible doctors I could have gotten at such a large training hospital. And the only one who could know what she knew. Just the right one . . . not a coincidence.

Looking back, I can't tell you specifically how this event figured in my early faith. I just knew from my parents that God had intervened in my life, and His care became part of my life narrative—that God was there and looks out for us in hard times. We can turn to Him. I had learned early what trauma was like . . . going from an active almost four-year-old to one day suddenly being told I could not walk anymore and would be in a wheelchair! It happened out of nowhere. Screaming "Why can't I walk?? Let me walk!" I remember the chaos of it all and the angry fits.

It was a really difficult time, for close to two years. I remember getting disciplined if I ever put one ounce of weight on that leg. I remember being in severe pain. Being disabled and not allowed to play like I could before, I was left out of many of the childhood activities that my friends would engage in. I remember sitting on the sidelines at birthday parties while the other children rode the pony, feeling like something was wrong with me. I was different somehow . . . flawed. Ashamed. I remember walking down stairs on my crutches and leg braces and tripping and falling down flights of stairs, stabbed by my crutches as they broke, bleeding on the steps of the post office. I remember the looks as I got on the bus with my crutches and people asking my nanny "What is wrong with the sick child?" I remember being called "Crip" and later having flashbacks of big, scary x-ray machines and medical procedures.

It was a difficult period for me and for our family and one that would have other psychological and emotional ramifications in my life. But the spiritual imprinting on me was powerful . . . that when there is tragedy and life is no longer like it was before, He is there.

I got well a couple of years later and returned to normal life. I put it all out of my head. Not wanting to be "crippled" anymore, I jumped headlong into the exact opposite: becoming a sports nut. I guess I was making up for lost time and trying to overcompensate for my physical insecurity, but I played every possible sport. I had to prove I was not "inferior" or just a "crippled" child. Football, baseball, basketball, golf, diving, karate, and more. At age eleven or twelve I won the Mississippi state diving championship, placed third in the Three State Southern Competition, and was asked to begin further training by Olympic coaches to prepare for becoming an Olympic diver one day. Later, I placed third in a karate championship from ten states. I was abnormally driven. But slowly, as I was too short for basketball and too small for football, golf was emerging as my sport, my passion, and soon it became my total life.

By age twelve, I knew that I loved golf more than anything else. I played all the tournaments, did well, and slowly gave up all other sports to pursue my passion. I was also involved in all the other activities of school, social life, the Southern life of hunting and fishing and water-skiing, and of course, pursuing girls. Over time the pain and trauma and the spiritual lesson I had learned through my earlier illness was all faded. It was another life. I had put being the "crippled" child very far in the past.

And as I moved on in life's pursuits, I kept God very private and personal—God was my friend, but I was not very involved with faith in a public way. I talked to God a lot, tried to stay close to Him, and pretty much kept that from everyone else.

Until I had no choice.

Two

Seek and You Will Find

Playing Junior Golf in Mississippi in those high school years was exciting. Not only because of the tournaments, the traveling, and the thrill of competition, but mostly for looking forward to the future: college. I was being recruited by different schools and had not made up my mind, when I got an invite from the coach at Southern Methodist University to come to Dallas and discuss playing there. I did not know a lot about SMU other than its football, but it was a great golf school. I accepted the invitation to go for a visit and play with the coach.

It is still a vivid memory, going to Dallas and playing at Northwood CC, a site where the PGA, one of the four majors, had been played. My golf teacher went with me, and after the day, the coach asked me to join the SMU golf team. I was ecstatic. The next step in my dream was coming true. That fall, I would be going to Dallas.

Upon arriving, I was stunned to find out that the coach had resigned abruptly that week and there was no new coach in place. An interim coach was put in, and since my promised scholarship was only partial the first semester and was not to go full until the second semester, the interim coach said that he was going to hit reset and we newbies would have to qualify for the team. I was stunned . . . I thought everything was secure, as it had been promised, and then I found I would have to make it all over again. I could have gone to several different great schools, but my heart was set on SMU by this time. So, I agreed to stay and play the qualifier. There were a lot of good players trying to qualify, and only two spots for the team. My entire college choice depended on that qualifying tournament. If I did not make it, I would then transfer to a school where I knew I could play.

I made it. I shot under par for the qualifier and two of us qualified on that final cold and rainy day in Dallas. I was relieved to say the least. My place on the team was secure.

Later that fall, I injured my wrist, and my play was hampered throughout the rest of the year. Sometimes I played well, and other times not at all. I went to several doctors, who struggled to diagnose my pain. They thought it was tendonitis and just gave me a lot of shots. By the next summer, things seemed to be looking up. I was getting cortisol shots, playing various tournaments, and continuing to push forward. I had a good summer, coming close to winning the Mississippi Open. I was two under par for the tournament, within two shots of the lead, when the tournament was called because of rain before the last day. But having less pain and winning some other tournaments that summer, I had great hopes for my sophomore year back at SMU.

The new coach who replaced the interim was a great one, Earl Stewart, a former tour player and Texas Hall of Fame recipient. He was really encouraging to me, and excited with me about how things were looking up that summer, and I'll always be grateful for how he helped me go through all of that. I still have a letter he wrote me that summer about all of the good that was happening and looking forward to the fall.

But as the fall came, the pain continued and increased. It was such a bummer . . . all of that preparation for years, hopes and dreams, and getting a chance to play at a great school as well. There were several All-Americans on the team, a great bunch of guys. Payne Stewart, who would go on to become a great player and US Open champion, was a teammate. One Payne story I remember vividly was right before the first week of school, Coach Stewart called me and said, "We have a new kid coming in, and he has no car. Can you pick him up at the airport and bring him to the course?" I said sure . . . and that kid was Payne.

I picked him up that day, and we went to play one of the courses we often played, and . . . right off the plane . . . onto the course . . . Payne shot some really low number, something like 65 or 67. That was impressive but not extremely unusual, as on a given day, any college player could have a good round. But this is what stood out: I knew that something was up with this kid that was more than just having a good round. I remember thinking that day, *This kid is different. He has something I have not seen.* Turns out that was more true than I even knew. He became one of the greats.

Since he did not have a car and I did, we often drove together to afternoon rounds and practice, and spent hours together on the practice range. What great memories . . . and what a good guy he was. When he died in a plane crash years later, it was heartbreaking to the golf world and to much of the country. The PGA Tour lost one of its greats, and everyone who knew him lost a great friend.

Through the spring of my sophomore year, my wrist pain worsened. I fought it, sometimes playing well but not well at others. I was beginning to lose hope of ever playing well again. And finally, after fighting it as long as I could, I called my dad and Coach Stewart and told them I was going to hang it up. It felt pointless to continue to fight trying to play when every backswing I did not know if I would have a knife shoot through my wrist or not. I felt devastated and yet somewhat relieved at the same time. Coach Stewart told me to come over to his house that night, and we talked. He wanted me to be well and continue and was encouraging, yet at the same time was very understanding and was aligned with my decision. Mixed feelings were all around.

But the battle for two years of playing with pain and struggling had taken its toll, and my quest in competitive golf for so many years had abruptly come to an end. As a kid, I had always thought I would have some kind of a career in golf . . . if not someday playing (which is every kid's dream), then I would be a club pro and a teacher. But my dream and my lifelong passion in golf up to that point was now over. Dead in the water, and I felt worse than dead myself.

To say that I was depressed would be an understatement. To lose golf was to lose what I thought my life was about. It also had a lot to do with losing something special with my dad. He had started me playing with him when I was a really little kid . . . riding with him and then taking it up more formally. It was something we shared deeply . . . he would always come to my tournaments and get more nervous than I would. It would kind of crack me up to see the pressure get to him, even when it was me playing.

Once, I was invited to play in the St. Jude Classic Pro Am in Memphis as a teenager. I remember going on to the range to warm up and was slotted between Lee Trevino and Gary Player, and Jack Nicklaus was a few players away. I thought my dad was going to faint, seeing his kid hitting balls with all of the great players of the time. And he was so nervous. But I remember being so happy to make him proud that day, as I shot six under par for the last sixteen holes, winning the Pro Am with partner Larry Ziegler. It was one of my fondest memories with my dad and golf. Losing my golf game meant losing something very special with him, and it hit me hard to tell him I was giving it up. I hated making that call. He was accepting of it and understood, but I know it was tough for him as well.

At the same time that I lost my golf game, my girlfriend and I broke up. So, here I was, twenty years old and, in my mind, a total washout. Depressed, and with no idea what my future held or what I even wanted to do. Those were very dark days. I struggled to find some sense of meaning, some purpose now that I had none. I know it sounds weird now to have taken all of this so seriously, as I was only twenty years old. How can your life be over at twenty? But, to me it was. Everything was just dark.

I struggled to get out of bed in the mornings and go to classes that held no future or promise for me. I was an accounting and finance major, but after that next summer working at a bank, I knew I did not want a career in finance. I had always entertained the thought that I would go to law school if I did not pursue some kind of career in professional golf, but a couple of semesters of business law had turned me off as I learned that so much of law was reading case briefs and precedent nuances that got tedious. I would get even more depressed when I would talk to my friends who knew what they were going to be doing, looking forward to med school, law school, business school, or some other particular plan or dream. All I had to look forward to, it seemed, was nothing but blackness. How in the world would I ever make a living?

I know now, as a psychologist, that not having a life purpose at that age was not the cause of my depression. It was the losses I had recently sustained that were sending me into an abyss. What I did not know at the time was that those losses were cracking a not very strong foundation of being a pretty wounded person underneath it all. As I would learn later, my obsessive pursuits of sports and academic achievements were covering a lot of pain that I had never faced from my growing-up years. I was a high-functioning time bomb of pain ready to crash, and losing golf was the trigger that sent me hurling into the black hole. The clinical term for those events is "precipitating factor." It means that often, when people go through something like a divorce, death of a loved one, loss of a job, etc., that pain will trigger deeper, unresolved issues that they have never dealt with, and they will feel it all at once. Often, this is why they cannot understand why "this," whatever "this" is, hurts so much. It seems like it is knocking them for a loop that it shouldn't. They feel, *Why can't I just get my act together?* All the while, they do not know that there is always a reason they feel the way they do and why they can't put it all back together by themselves. That was me.

I would spend my days looking for some kind of purpose, something that would make me want to dive into life again. But I just couldn't find it. At first, I had thought it might be a good opportunity to pursue things I had never had time to pursue, since I had basically lived on the golf course since I was a young kid. And I did pursue them that year, but they held no pleasure or promise. Of course, I did not know that that is one of the symptoms of clinical depression, "anhedonia." It is the inability to derive pleasure from anything in life, even if it is something you love. Your chemical and emotional state will not allow it. I should have been in a hospital, knowing what I know now. But I just tried to white-knuckle it and make it one more day, acting the best I knew how to act and prove to everyone around me that I was okay. But I wasn't. I wished I could go to sleep and never wake up. Every morning, within a few seconds of waking up, the heavy blackness would descend like a ton of bricks, and I had no hope for that day being any different from the one before.

That is where I was one Sunday afternoon in my dorm room at SMU, sitting on my bed, staring into nothing, everything dark. There was a merry-go-round of questions going through my head. How do you get undepressed when nothing you try works? How does someone find what they want to do in life when literally nothing interests you? How do you get energy to go on when you feel like you can't get out of bed in the morning or throughout the day? How do you find the right relationship? And, once you do, how do you make it work and make a commitment? How would I make a living and pay for the life I wanted? How would I get a job, and what career would interest me? How would I ever achieve "success"? The questions seemed to be a whir in my head at that moment sitting on my bed . . . when it happened.

I looked across the room and my eyes somehow were drawn to my Bible. I had taken it to school, but had not opened it since I had arrived. The faith of my childhood seemed to be very far off and was certainly not helping me. But this moment, something was drawing me to that book. It was as if it stood out from the shelf in some way. I could say it almost "called" me, it felt. I still remember the moment.

So I went over and got it and sat back down. I had no idea what I was doing, other than thinking, *I wonder if this will help.* Not knowing where to turn or what to read, I randomly opened it up. I looked down at the page, and a passage sort of leaped off the page:

> ***Seek first the kingdom of God and His righteousness and all these things shall be added to you.*** (Matthew 6:33 NKJV)

Wait . . . what?? Let me read that again. I did, and I realized what it was saying to me. Right as I was worrying and obsessing about "all these things," it said that if I would seek God (whatever that meant), that all of this other stuff would work out? All of this life stuff that I had no clue how to solve? Really?

At this point, I had no faith at all that was making me believe everything would be okay or that God had it all in control. I was depressed and just wanted to either die or somehow hit reset. I was so far from believing that God actually did things in our lives that I had no idea that this could be true. That there was a real God who would help me make my life work? I believed in God, but had never really tested whether or not He would be active in my life and actually intervene and do things. Really? Was that possible?

But I had tried everything else, so . . . why not?

"Okay," I thought. "I'll try this."

I had no clue how it was supposed to work. God was someone I had talked to in my life and had even loved and felt close to, but not in any way such that I actually thought He would solve my problems.

What was I supposed to do? The verse said "seek," so I decided to do that.

I didn't think you could really seek God in a dorm room. I felt you needed a church. So I went outside and walked over to the little chapel across from the dorm, Perkins Chapel there at SMU. It was a cold, dark Sunday afternoon, but the chapel was open and I went in. It was dark and dreary—so quiet and lonely. I walked down to the altar, knelt down on my knees, and said something like this: "God, I really don't even know if You are really there. I believe You are, but I don't really know. But I need help. Please . . . help me. Just help me. Please . . . show me You are there and help me. And if You do, I will do whatever You want me to do. I just need You to do something."

There. I had done it. I had reached out to God with all I knew to do. It was like jumping out of an airplane with a parachute and hoping the chute would open. I had believed in God and felt like I really loved Him and talked to him, but this was different: This time I *needed* Him. I had tried everything, and nothing was working. This was, it seemed, my last hope.

And then . . . nothing. Nothing happened. Silence.

It was devastating.

I had seen on TV that when people "turn to God," they got zapped . . . or something. Something was supposed to happen with you gave it all to Him. When you really jumped out of the plane, the parachute would open. But nothing did. Zero. Just silence.

I remember feeling the most alone I had ever felt. I had done it and got nothing in return. I felt so alone and hopeless, because I knew if He was not there, I had no clue what I was going to do to get out of his hole.

So, I just stood there in silence, looking at the high ceiling. I thought or muttered something like "So . . . call me."

And I went back to my dorm feeling more hopeless than when I had entered. God had not shown up.

Three

The Phone Call

I went back to my dorm room, and I wish I could remember the timeline. I don't know if it happened right that moment or a little later that day. But I do vividly remember the call. The phone rang, and it was my fraternity brother, Ed Atkinson. He said something like this: "Okay, I don't know what made me think of you, but I did, so I am calling to tell you we are starting a Bible study at the fraternity house, and I wanted to see if you would want to come."

Now, you might think this was a coincidence. But all I can tell you is that I hoped it was not. I really thought it was an answer. I thought, *This has to be a sign*. Little did I know how that call would forever change my life.

I went to the Bible study, and it was being led by Ed's brother-in-law, Bill. Bill was a seminary student and seemed to know what he was talking about, and I liked it. But after attending several meetings and still being depressed, I knew that I needed to talk to Bill more about what I had been going through, so I asked him to meet me for lunch. I told him how depressed I had been, and how it seemed like God had not been doing anything for me when I had prayed for help with my depression. He just said, "Keep coming to the study. Sometimes God has his own timing, and he uses people, too. He can use the group to help you as you learn more about Him."

That seemed like such a cop-out to me. I wanted God to do something, like write something across the sky, or touch me supernaturally and make me feel better. Or show me what to do, dammit! Didn't He see that I was desperate? Do something! All I got was "Keep coming . . . God uses people, too." What a lame God . . . it seemed to me. But I had no other choice, so I kept coming back, as they say in AA.

As I did, I found that several things were happening at once. First, what I was hearing in the study created a conflict for me in my classes at school. My classes were telling me that the Bible was a bunch of myths . . . that we came from the Big Bang exploding a primordial pile of goo and we even had no reason for the "goo" to exist. They said that Sigmund Freud said that God was only a wish fulfillment for a father to make it all better, and many other academic tear-downs of faith. I felt like I had stepped into quicksand . . . so I did what the Bible study was teaching me to do when we have questions and doubts: pray. So, I asked God about each question that I would encounter. That was when I began to see that God is active, and answers prayer.

It was my first step into a journey that has never stopped . . . reaching out to God when I hit a wall and finding that He was there. I would ask Him about those questions, and the answer would appear. I was finding out the most important thing that I want you to know: *God answers our prayers and our questions.* I had questions about science and the Bible, evolution, the Flood, quantum physics, astronomy and cosmology, biology, philosophy, archaeology, theology, the existence of evil, pain and suffering, and the like. I was swamped with questions . . . and each time, an answer would appear at some point that would make the questions go away. The answers were more than satisfactory.

I found that there were astrophysicists, PhD professors in biology, cosmology, geology, archaeology, and all of the sciences who believed for scientific reasons that science did not go against their faith but in fact proved their faith. I made it a search to learn all that I could learn, and after a time, the questions dissolved. I found out, from scientists themselves, that there is no scientific reason to not have faith.

Science can only observe what is, what *already* exists . . . it cannot observe what does not exist, nor can it observe or know where what does exist came from. It can build theories to explain it . . . and have "faith" in its theories, but it cannot know any more about where it all came from than just to have its own "faith" that the material world was "eternal," and then somehow developed into "life." It cannot explain why the material or physical matter of the universe always existed, or if it didn't, how it suddenly did. How we got "something from nothing." Nor can it explain why the intricate interworkings (the design) of everything that exists works together and as well as it does. And as we will see, what science did observe supported my faith very well.

There are many, many great resources for you to explore those questions on your own, if you need to, as I did. My purpose here is not to write a "science and the Bible" book, but a book to share with you why I have faith. And my main point at this juncture is to share with you that each time I would have a question, He would give me an answer that sufficed. God either answered it specifically, or answered something bigger than that particular question that made the original question moot.

I was finding out that what the Bible said was true:

> ***Seek, and you will find.*** (Matthew 7:7 NKJV)
>
> ***You will seek me and find me when you seek me with all your heart*** (Jeremiah 29:13 CSB)

Each step of the way, as I sought Him, He gave me the answers I needed, or showed me that I didn't really need them after all. I just needed Him. I was learning that a relationship with Him would provide what I needed in the areas of questions I had. But I still had what felt like a much bigger problem.

I was still depressed.

And two things were becoming clear to me: God was answering prayers, *and* not answering them. He was showing me that he was real, but not really healing my depression. I went home for the summer, with a new faith, and a lot of depression and mental anguish. What I didn't know was that it was going to get worse before it got better.

Four

Into the Abyss, and out of Egypt

For the rest of the spring, I sought God with all that I had. I read everything I could put my hands on about the evidence for the faith of Jesus, and also about spiritual growth. And some of the most powerful reading I did was about the reality of God's being there for people. I found a whole new world of literature that I never knew existed: spiritual biographies and testimonies. People writing about what God actually had done in their lives, work and missions. There were some amazing books and programs that I found where people told their stories of God's real interventions into their lives. I found out I was not imagining the reality of His intervening into our worlds . . . countless others had testimonies of the same. Healings, provision, intervention, guidance . . . I was dumbfounded that I had lived so long and was so unaware of how alive God was in the real world.

One of the first ones that really affected me was *The Cross and the Switchblade*, by David Wilkerson. It was the story of a small-town preacher in Pennsylvania whom God visited in the middle of the night and told him to go to NYC to rescue some gang members accused of horrible crimes. I had no idea that God did supernatural things still . . . I knew the Bible talked about them, but I had never heard much about those things happening today.

Another book I remember reading in those beginning days of my journey was *God's Smuggler*, by Brother Andrew. It was the story of how he smuggled Bibles into communist countries and the miracles of God's protection and intervention. These two books and many others showed me something I didn't understand before—that *God is alive and will enter and intervene in our lives.*

While growth in my faith was going well, finding my way out of the darkness of depression was not. I went home to Mississippi from Dallas for the summer, and decided that since so much of my pain was associated with losing so much at SMU, and I didn't know what I wanted to study or pursue, I decided to transfer to Ole Miss. I thought, at least for a semester, I would like a change of scenery and maybe something would click. In retrospect, I was running from all of the pain, which was probably not a bad idea.

As the summer was continued, everything just got worse. Even concentrating was difficult. I was working at a bank as a teller, and sometimes just could not focus enough to do my work. I kept making small errors that made no sense. One day it all came to a head when I mistakenly wrapped a stack of $50 bills in a $1 bill wrapper and gave it to a woman who was making a withdrawal. I thought I was handing her fifty $1 bills, since the wrapper said "1s," and in reality I gave her fifty $50 bills. She won the "pick a depressed teller" lottery and never came back, and I lost my job.

It was during that time of extreme struggle that I experienced my first supernatural experience. In a despondent moment, while losing my job, I went for a drive up to my family's lake house, where I used to talk to God as a teenager. I thought I might somehow feel close to Him there like I did sometimes in high school. What I didn't know was that He was looking to be close to me.

I was driving in my car on the deeply wooded road to the lake, talking to God, when He came into and throughout my entire being in the most powerful way I know to describe. It felt like I was being supercharged with some kind of energy, and that energy was lifting me up into some kind of high that I never had felt. As a psychologist, if I heard this from someone, I might think they were having a manic episode, but I wasn't. My thinking, impulse control, reality orientation, mental status, etc. were all fine, and afterward the depression was still around. I could have passed any mental status exam at that moment. I wasn't bipolar, vacillating from a depressive low to having some kind of manic high psychosis. I knew it was God somehow touching me, and what I was sensing from the experience was *He is just showing me that He is with me.* It was such a strong showing of His being with me is all I know to say, so strong that I remember telling Him, "Okay! That is enough! *Stop!*" It felt as if it would be too much if it were any stronger. I felt like I might be ejected out of my car or go nuts. And after a while, it just left. I went back home and to my depressed, struggling world. But I had been touched by Him, and somehow . . . encouraged.

It was so amazing to have experienced that touch so strongly on the one hand, and on the other hand, it was so confusing to *still* be in a bad place. God didn't heal me at that moment. But I learned a valuable twofold lesson that would serve me for the rest of my life: *God is with us even when things are really bad. Just because they are bad does not mean that He is not with us. And just because He is with us does not mean that He removes all of the bad stuff right then.* I later saw that He says this in the Bible so many times, in so many ways. One of my favorite verses is this one:

> ***Even though I walk through the darkest valley, I will fear no evil, for you are with me; your rod and your staff, they comfort me.*** (Psalm 23:4)

I was learning something important that was breaking through my nascent and immature spiritual life . . . God allows us to go through pain, and pain does not mean that He does not care or is not with us. I could not deny reality at this point . . . I *knew* He was there. There was no escaping that, and at the same time I knew that for some reason He was allowing me to still be in a bad place. Both of those were true. It was a tough pill to swallow, but it did give me the faith to continue to walk forward and pursue whatever He had for me, and trust Him for the first time in a new way.

The summer progressed, and at some point I made a trip to Ole Miss to get registered and signed in. On the way there, I was feeling worse and worse. I was more depressed and also beginning to experience lots of what felt like overwhelming fear. It was an overall dread and fear that something bad was going to happen even though I couldn't name it. I now know it was just more of the depression and comorbid anxiety (as is often the case with depression), as well as, I would later learn, some PTSD reactions from my childhood illness. But as I arrived in Oxford, I was feeling swamped by it all.

But there was one experience that was another proof to me that God was still there and with me. I was at a registration table at Ole Miss where many students were signing up for classes, rooms, etc. I was barely able to concentrate in my depression and anxiety, finding it difficult to even fill out the information forms. In the midst of all of that confusion, a man walked up to me out of the blue, looked at me, and said something like this: "God is with you, and one day you are going to be a great man of God, serving him in big ways." I looked at him like he was nuts . . . I could not imagine doing anything of value for God or anyone else at that moment. I could barely get through the day. But it was like God saw me and told me once again, "Keep walking. I am with you." That was enough to keep me going one more day. I knew that God had spoken to me through that man . . . seeing me even though I couldn't even see my next steps.

Things kept getting worse, and a couple of weeks later, as the fall was approaching, a revival was taking place at a church in my town. It seemed like it was the kind of place where they believed in God healing people. Unlike my normal, regular Methodist church, this place prayed for people at the end of services and believed that God would do "stuff." I felt like I needed some of that, so I went. Maybe I would finally get "zapped."

I listened to the sermon, and felt moved, but did not really engage in the service enough to go up to the altar and ask for prayer or anything like that. I kind of kept a bit incognito.

But I sensed that the pastor was the real thing . . . I sensed that he actually believed in a God who would do things, who would actually intervene in our lives and help us.

The next day or so, I was in a really bad place. I prayed to God to help me, and suddenly, that pastor came to mind. I knew somehow I had to get to him. The church was closed and so I did not know how to find him, but I just *knew* that he was the one I was supposed to talk to. But . . . how would I find him? I *knew* I needed to talk to him ASAP, but had no way of finding him. So . . . I just prayed: "God, take me to him."

I remembered that my dad had said he thought he lived in a certain section of town . . . nothing specific, mind you, but a general area north of the city. That's all the direction I had. So, I asked God to take me to him. (You can see how desperate I was . . . that's so random!)

But I began to drive, and I don't know how to describe it, but at each intersection in that end of town that I came to, I felt some prompting to "turn left" or "turn right." I just kept doing it, for quite a while. It was about twenty minutes away.

I was getting deeper and deeper into a subdivision development north of town, following the promptings, street after street, when I made one more turn. *Suddenly, I felt the atmosphere in my car totally change.* Tangibly. The very air changed. I *knew* God had entered my car. I could feel the most incredible Presence surrounding me. I stopped the car at that instant. Then, I looked up, and there was a mailbox on the street in front of a house. It said, simply, "Rev. Jenkins." I had literally been led directly to the pastor's house. And God's presence in the car was undeniable.

I have only felt that kind of overwhelming presence a few times in my life, but it said something very powerful to me: God is *way* more real and near than we know. And He will intervene and help us.

I knocked on his door, and Rev. Jenkins graciously took me in and began to listen to all of my misery and dilemmas. I was thinking that since God had led me to him so specifically, he would somehow make it all go away, either through a healing, or some sort of counseling. Yet again, that did not happen. But what did happen through him was really a significant next step.

I broke down further that evening with Reverend Jenkins. I was so bad off that he called my parents to come get me. He did not know what to do . . . I was so broken and unable to get myself together that he was at the end of his skills. But he knew, wisely, that I needed more help. He told my parents that I needed psychiatric help, that I was chemically depressed and needed a doctor. He started the process that would lead me in the right direction.

Much like when I was four years old and my parents were at their wits' end, they took me back to the Oschner clinic in New Orleans, the place where you take the hard cases. They checked me in, and I was assigned a psychiatrist. I won't mention his name, but I can tell you now—and this is my professional opinion—he was inept. And at the same time, grandiosely confident. He completely misdiagnosed me, put me on the wrong medicine, and started down a course of therapy that had very little to do with what I was dealing with. He just did not understand me. The medicine was also producing some significant side effects and making me worse, and nothing was looking good. I felt *so* abandoned by God, and by my parents as well. Wrongly, since they were doing all they knew to do, but here I was, alone in a hospital 225 miles from home, missing the beginning of the school year, having no plan and no hope. I did not know what to do or where to turn.

There were a few bright spots that summer, further supernatural evidence that God was at work in my life, guiding me and protecting me. One stands out in my memory. My sister, who lived in New Orleans at the time, came to visit one day, and we went out to the French Quarter in New Orleans just to get me out and about and have a normal day. We were walking around, looking at various shops, when I saw an antique bookstore I wanted to visit. I was really into books, especially spiritual ones, as I was still searching. So, we were about to enter the bookstore when it happened. *God's presence fell all over us*. Yes, that is what I said, and I know it sounds crazy.

It was *so* powerful . . . He was enveloping us there on the sidewalk. Very much like that experience I had had in the car. I knew for sure it was Him.

I did not know why . . . but I said to Sharon, "Stop . . . we need to pray." And I just said, "God, I know you are here . . . please let me know why You are here and what to do." I had no idea what was going on. Sharon just looked at me like I was a bit crazy, but she trusted me. I didn't get any answer when I prayed, just His presence.

Still not knowing what this was about, we walked into the bookstore and just began to look around. I could still feel the Presence around me, but I just continued shopping. As I said, I am a book freak . . . so I love old bookstores. So, we wandered through the bookshelves, looking. I turned down another row of shelves and noticed a different section that was all spiritual books of various kinds. That tall row of bookcases caught my attention, and the first one I saw was a book by Hal Lindsey. I just stopped because I recognized the author as a Christian author. But when I stopped, all of a sudden, a very creepy man dressed in all black stepped suddenly in front of me and said with a very creepy tone, "Ahhh . . . so you are a Satanist?"

What I had not seen was the book Lindsey had written called *Satan Is Alive and Well on Planet Earth*. It was a book about Satan, and apparently, when I stopped to look at it, this satanist saw me and figured I was on his team.

I immediately felt *very* empowered and emboldened in some strange way . . . and said, "No! I am a Christian!" Normally I am not so ballistic as I felt in that encounter . . . but I felt a bit like a superhero. I later recognized that the power was not from myself. It even scared my sister.

When I said that, he drew back and recoiled . . . and said in the most hideous voice, "*Oh!* You are from the *wrong side*!" and then quickly moved away. In remembering it now, I want to say he almost *slithered* away. "Creepy" does not begin to describe the encounter.

Sharon was getting a bit freaked out, and grabbed me in the midst of the aftermath of the encounter and said, "Let's get out of here."

We walked outside, and then the Presence just left. Everything felt back to normal. It was weird to have felt it so strongly and then have it just gone. He was there, and then He wasn't. But I had learned another lesson: when I needed Him, He showed up. There was not a doubt that I was encountering some dark power that day, and God protected me from something, shielded me from things that I can only imagine. Decades later, having experienced real spiritual darkness and entities, even in clinical settings, I know that getting close to it is not something anyone wants to do unless they really know what they are doing.

But my experience taught me that God does protect. I later learned several verses that speak to what I had just witnessed, but here is one of my favorites:

> ***The Lord will protect you from all evil; He will keep your life. The Lord will guard your going out and your coming in [everything that you do] from this time forth and forever.*** (Psalm 121:7–8 AMP)

Sharon and I were amazed at how God had shown up in that moment, and it was just one more example of how He was with me . . . *even when I was otherwise incapacitated.* He shielded me. It may be that I was surrounded by angels . . . I don't know. I just know that I felt some really good support from a totally "other" dimension . . . one that I could not see but was learning was very, very real.

Before I move on and get to the next step of His plan for my healing, I want to just mention one more thing that might sound really, really strange to some of you, but all I can tell you is the truth. It was real, and it was very encouraging to me at the time.

When I was in the hospital waiting and hoping for Dr. Didn'tKnowWhatHeWasDoing to help me, every day there were occupational therapy sessions to engage in while I was just hanging out waiting for the doctor. I am not very artistic, so I decided to make a leather belt . . . and it was the kind of craft where you could emboss anything you wanted onto the leather. As a new Christian with a lot of zeal, I decided that I needed some "Jesus junk," so I started making a belt that had Jesus' name engraved into the leather. (I know . . . that sounds pretty cheesy, but I was a sophomore and it was the late seventies, so give me a break. Think hippies and the Jesus revolution, the Doobie Brothers, etc. ☺) Anyway, as I began to carve out his name—and I know no other way to describe this—every time I would work on the leather and see the name Jesus, I could literally feel a power coming from those words out of the leather. It was as if God was saying "This is true . . . His Power is real." I could literally feel it as if it was emanating from the leather itself. Call me crazy if you want . . . I probably would if I were you, and call it a hallucination. But I was not psychotic. I have to tell you the truth. It was real and I could *feel* it. Think holding your hand over a burner on a hot stove. And it sustained me several times with more hope to get through that very troubling time. I could *feel* Him. But in terms of my depression, I was still getting nowhere. My dunce of a psychiatrist was not helping me. Nothing was getting me to some sort of relief. I was alone in New Orleans with no support, and my parents were at the end of their rope. I was in some of the deepest despair that I had known yet . . . there just seemed to be no way forward.

Then, it happened. A nurse came to me and said I had a phone call. It was my friend Edward . . . the same friend who had invited me to that Bible study back at SMU. He had found out from my parents that I was there and said that he was coming to visit me. I suddenly felt like God had not forgotten me with nothing happening.

Edward calling seemed like a ray of light through the darkness. It was like God's calvary was coming, since he was the one who had started it all after my initial calling out to God.

Edward arrived the next day. Edward, he was a pretty "take no prisoners" kind of guy, and in his typical mode, he decided "these people are idiots. We need to get you to someone who understands your faith [my psychiatrist thought my faith was part of the problem] and can help you medically." So, he called his brother-in-law Bill, the seminary student who had led that first Bible study I had gone to at the Beta house at SMU. Bill was taking counseling courses at seminary from a psychiatrist named Dr. Frank Minirth, and Edward thought maybe Dr. Minirth could help.

Edward explained my situation to Bill. So, Bill put in a call to Dr. Minirth and asked if he could see me. Miraculously, Dr. Minirth said yes. The problem was that I had nowhere to stay in Dallas. If I went to Dallas, where would I stay? Again, God intervened. Julie, Bill's wife and Edward's sister, had been saying to Bill for a few weeks that she felt like God was telling her "someone was supposed to come live with us." This felt out of the blue to Bill. But Julie was absolutely convinced it was from God, and as they prayed about it, they both came to the realization that indeed God was telling them to prepare a place in their home for a guest. They had had no idea who or why, until that moment. When Edward called them to ask about my coming there to see Dr. Minirth, they looked at each other, and Bill said, "This is him. This is who is supposed to come live with us."

So Bill and Julie invited me to Dallas and see Dr. Minirth and live with them. A graduate student and his wife with a fourteen-month-old baby in a very tiny house and overloaded in every way were certain they were supposed to do this, as little rational sense as it made. They did not even have an extra bed in the little storeroom of a room where they would put me. But they said yes to what God was leading them to do.

They then called my parents to explain the plan, and my parents, for some crazy and strange reason, said yes. One more funny sign was the next day a friend of Julie's was cleaning out her garage and called them, saying "I am about to throw out a single bed but thought for some reason y'all might be able to use it. Do you want it?" They knew who that came from. The next day, I checked out, and went back to Dallas to move in with Bill and Julie. Dallas was where my misery had begun, and now I was going back there. Little did I know, my new life was truly about to begin.

I moved in with Bill and Julie. Bill took me to seminary classes with him. At times, I was still too depressed to concentrate or unable to go altogether. But at other times, I was eager to learn all of the basics of the faith and of the spiritual life. Most days, I would be at home with Julie and their toddler, Billy, and she would, day by day, principle by principle, teach me about God. I was getting a spiritual education, like I lived in my own residential seminary. But what I did not know was that as I was learning about God and how He heals our lives, He was doing it at the same time. I was not in a residential seminary; I was in a residential seminary/treatment center. Way better than the hospital I had been in. Bill and Julie sent me to see Dr. Minirth for my sessions, then they helped me process through what was taking place in my sessions. Bill also put a small group together for me: Edward, our good friend Fred, and a couple of other guys. Went deep into our lives, sharing pains and struggles, praying for each other, processing girlfriend pain and drama, sharing our fears for our futures, our difficulties in school, confessing our sins, and sometimes crying together about painful issues. One minute we might be talking about my losses, and next we would be talking about a parent who had to go into drug rehab or another whose mom had a nervous breakdown and the family was in crisis. We loved, supported, and healed one another in that small community that Bill and Julie had stewarded.

This time in my life was my season of being led through the wilderness. The biblical narrative is expressed well in a mini sermon by Moses in Deuteronomy, before the Israelites were about to enter the Promised Land, following their Exodus from Egypt. I was always able to relate to this story . . . as I think most people can. We all have our own bad experiences, our "Egypt's" that we need to be delivered from. And many have attested, as I have, to God's ability to bring us out of our own bad seasons to a better place, if we allow Him. My biggest "Egypt" was the struggles I have shared so far. When I look back on this season of my life, I can now say what Moses said: God brought me out with a mighty hand . . . he performed miracles . . . and gave me a land (a life) that I could never have found on my own. And He has taught me "statutes," or His "ways," as they are often referred to, and as I have learned, they have transformed my entire life.

Being led out of Egypt took the Israelites on a long trip, and I found my trip to be long as well, as He began my journey to healing.

All through that fall with Bill and Julie, I was still very much coming through the desert. In fact, even though I was back in Dallas beginning in late August, I did not enroll in the fall semester at SMU. I was still too fragile to function and carry an academic load. In fact, that small group of guys were the only people outside of Bill and Julie that I could even see or be around. I did not even look like myself. I had lost about thirty pounds and would have scared people, I think. I am sure many would have thought I had some terminal disease. I was afraid of the questions that would naturally ensue.

And I still wanted so much for God to "heal me," to "zap" me, and make it all go away. But He wasn't doing that. There were still some really hard times. But healing times at the same time.

One such example was as Christmas approached that year. Bill and Julie and I were watching a movie adaptation of *A Christmas Carol*, by Charles Dickens. You may remember Tiny Tim from the story—Bob Cratchit's crippled son, who was in danger of dying from his illness, which had rendered him unable to walk without a crutch. We were just all sitting in their den, watching the movie on TV, everything normal, when Tiny Tim entered the scene on his crutches.

As he did, out of the blue, I began to hyperventilate. I began to shake and tremble. Then, I began to have flashbacks of my childhood illness and of being that crippled kid . . . images of hospitals, people in white coats, loud x-ray machines, needles . . . It was like a whirling collage of terrifying pictures cascading through my head.

I began to sob. Bill and Julie surrounded me and just held me until I could talk about what was happening. Slowly, I came around. And we processed it all pretty deeply. What I did not understand at the time that I was having PTSD symptoms from the physical pain and trauma and the emotional damage that was done in those two years beginning around my fourth birthday. The illness that God had rescued me from through Dr. Sherman had been physically healed, *but* it had been lurking in my soul and psyche for all those years. I later understood that part of my breakdown in losing my ability to play golf was a big trigger that had sent me whirling into the pits of all the darkness that lay beneath. I was not just depressed over not being able to play competitive golf. I was reliving what had never healed of underneath it all. The current loss was unearthing my buried childhood trauma and losses.

There were several other losses from my childhood and some physical abuse that emerged, which I began to process as well that year. I had wanted God to "heal" me, to "zap" me in an immediate flash of supernatural power—I had wanted Him to do that from the first day I turned to Him in that little chapel. But He didn't. So I thought He wasn't going to. I had to just learn to walk in faith and cope as best I could. I was learning to lean on Him for strength and was grateful to God for what I had seen Him do and how He had shown up, but I was disappointed that He was not healing me.

But the reality was that He was healing me at a much deeper level than I had been wanting . . . just to not be depressed anymore. He was taking me through a deeper more thorough healing of my soul in these healing relationships. He was repairing me from the ground up.

Bill and Julie, Dr. Minirth, and my close spiritual community were working me over while I thought God was not "healing" me. They were supporting me, doing surgery in my soul as they made me process a lot of what was surfacing in therapy, grieving losses. They were also tough on me . . . they confronted me (lovingly) on patterns in my life that were not healthy. They dug around in my soul. They made me confess and bring to the light crummy attitudes, unforgiveness I carried, relational patterns I had, my performance orientation in life to prove myself. It was not all milk and cookies by any means. This was a tough treatment team.

I remember one day when I was beginning to entertain going back on campus and afraid of what some people might think. They would know that I had been through a hard time. Julie just looked me in the eye and said point blank, "Henry . . . that's just pride." Her brutal honesty helped me take another step out of my lack of vulnerability with people, and my tendency to worry about what people would think if they knew I had struggled so badly. My first class in "being real."

I was learning the psychological, and biblical, construct of the "true self" and the "false self." I had built a false self that I began to show the outside world when I crawled out of that wheelchair and was going to prove that I was not an inferior, crippled child. I was going to be an athlete. Every sport I could play, accomplishing state championships and regional championships in some, getting recruited to play NCAA golf. I was not cripple anymore . . . my false self had done its job. It kept the crippled child hidden, buried where no one would know. Or so I thought.

What psychology and later the Bible taught me was that a false self, which covers up who we really are, is a house built on sand. It will ultimately crash, and I was finding that to be more than true. Jesus called it being a "hypocrite," a term that literally meant "actor." One would go to the theater to see the "hypocrites" perform. The apostle Paul said the same thing, that we should "put off falsehood" (Ephesians 4:25 NKJV). My false self had cracked, and it was all coming to the surface, the truth that I was running from, long since forgotten. But PTSD does not lie, and trophies won't hide it. Julie was essentially telling me, "Give it up. Be true to yourself, God, and others." Another healing swipe of the scalpel that was very present throughout that year, but healing, as it was done in love.

I will talk more about the biblical processes that psychology has proven empirically to be true, but what I did not know was that God was doing them throughout that entire year.

Support, grief, uncovering things, processing pain, healing brokenheartedness, strengthening, modeling, risk taking, weeping together, confession, forgiveness, repentance, changing thinking patterns, life examination and moral inventories, prayer, building new skills, and many more. They were all happening, and I had no clue. I was just "waiting for God to heal me." And since I was not able to "perform" and hide anymore, I was on the surgery table with no other choice. The false self had been dismantled.

About a year later after my time with Bill and Julie, I was feeling pretty good. I had reentered college life and enrolled at SMU to continue there for my last two years. I was living in an apartment with Edward and another friend, had a new direction in life, a great spiritual community, had reconnected with my fraternity buddies, was dating again, and was feeling good about life. I had hope and a future.

I woke up one morning and was aware of something pretty startling . . . it had not really hit me in full force until that moment. This thought shot through my mind:

I am not depressed anymore.

It was true. I wasn't depressed. I felt pretty good.

As I lay there letting that awareness sink in, thinking of all of the good things in my life at that point, I was so full and grateful to be this alive again. I was thanking God for all the people and direction I had now in my life. Then I had a thought:

But I wish God had healed me.

I was disappointed that the God I had found had not healed me. I had not gotten "zapped" with a supernatural healing, making my depression go away. I lay there for a bit, kind of bummed that He had not done it.

Then a verse hit me, and I read it again, with that thought in mind:

> ***From him the whole body, joined and held together by every supporting ligament, grows and heals itself up in love, as each part does its work.*** (Ephesians 4:16)

Wait . . . "From him"? From Jesus? "The whole body?" (meaning His body of followers, His people)? As they are connected and each part does their work, we are healed?

I was kind of speechless, embarrassed, and touched. I realized that was exactly what had happened to me. Jesus had connected me through supporting ligaments—his people—held me together, and healed me as each part had done its work. Julie, Bill, my doctor, my other friends who did all of those healing things were the "parts" of His body healing me just like the human body heals.

The "head," our brain, directs the kidneys and liver to clean us out, the heart pumps new oxygenated blood out to where it is needed, food is broken down and metabolized to send nutrients and materials that turn into new cells, the immune system fights the infection, and so forth. I realized something.

Jesus did that through Bill and Julie and others. He had designed the whole experience. They cleaned out and flushed out my infections in my soul, fought off the bacteria that were inside of me, strengthened my bones and put them back in place, took new material to the parts of me that were missing what I needed, and more. And all the time, the "Head" was directing it. I realized it:

God did heal me.

But he hadn't done it through a zapping. He had done it through a phone call that started the process and invited me out of my Egypt, putting me in the initial group that explained Jesus to me, brought person after person to answer my questions and Bible dilemmas, supernaturally sustained me with visitations on the road in a car, on Bourbon Street in New Orleans, in a hospital, became an invisible GPS to get me to a stranger pastor's house, led me to the need for professional help, sent Edward to rescue me from my hospital prison, provided the doctor who knew what I needed, supernaturally spoke to the perfect young couple to take me into their home, provided them with the knowledge and skills to love me back into health, started breaking my PTSD down, placed me in a healing community and more.

I had to face the facts: God did heal me. And as he did it, I did not really even see all of what He was doing, because of my pain. But that morning I did, and then I knew something more . . . if He had healed me in a miraculous, supernatural moment, I would not have begun the long path of growing up, and growing out of some very immature and broken patterns that were keeping me stuck and would have literally plagued me for life. If He had not done it His way, I probably would be living in a gutter right now with a trail of broken relationships and many other failures. Still immature and broken underneath a zapping of the "depression" that I thought was the real problem.

So, lesson learned.

God is real, and He cares. But sometimes we don't know what He is doing while we are wandering around the desert for what feels like forty years, as Moses' people did. He visited them, was leading them, and they were still struggling. They were griping, and could not often see that He was really doing anything. But He was . . . and He was with me. I was learning that God knows better than I do what I need, and He was bringing it to pass . . . even if was slow, almost invisible, and not doing it my way. But, looking back, I cannot deny the reality of what He did for me in the beginning of my journey. The building blocks of what I have wanted to share with you, the "why I believe," were slowly stacking up, and there were more dramatic ones still to come.

Five

A Leap of Faith

Facing the next year, the darkness had gone, and I was at a place to begin contemplating "what now?" I was an accounting and finance major, but slowly realizing that it was not grabbing me. I had always done my schoolwork, and loved business, but the subject matter seemed more laborious than engaging. Valuable information to know, especially if I did decide to do my forever fallback, which was go to law school. But I had to admit, I wasn't thrilled about any of it. A semester of business law and the idea of reading precedents and briefs and contracts for the next forty-plus years put me to sleep. Plus, my first job in the financial world, working at the bank the summer before, had ended in disaster. I got fired. Wasn't really a good omen that I belonged in that world.

What I was noticing, though, was literally all of my free time was spent voraciously reading theology books, and my newest passion, psychology. I had gotten interested in it along the way trying to read my way out of my pain. I was reading a lot of books on depression, anxiety, and related topics. Books that integrated spiritual growth and psychology held my interest especially. I devoured them. I pursued them with a similar zeal to how I had formerly pursued working on my golf game. The intersection of psychology and theology was becoming a passion.

I was noticing something else, too. In hang time with my friends, and with Bill and Julie and my group, when we were discussing the dynamics of our lives, and especially theirs, my mind was kicking into gear in a way I had never felt before. I was seeing things that I had never noticed before, figuring out dilemmas and the issues that people were dealing with. I also had empathy for people's pain, after what I had experienced. And I seemed to come alive inside when talking to people about their lives.

Then, slowly at first but then what seemed like all at once, person after person started saying things like "You seem to see things in these discussions that others don't see. And you also seem to be able to relate the Bible to all of it in ways that others don't, too. Have you ever thought about becoming a psychologist?"

About the same time, Dr. Minirth began to ask me the same thing, saying that he saw an aptitude in me in those same ways. One day, he just said point blank, "I think you should either go to medical school and become a psychiatrist or get a PhD in clinical psychology." I was a bit stunned. I had looked up to him, and now he was telling me that he thought I could do what he did. I felt a bit like I had instantly lost all respect for him, thinking that a klutz like me could actually do that. He must not be as smart as I thought he was. At the same time, it was a bit like Jack Nicklaus telling someone they should become a tour player. It hit me hard . . . like maybe I should listen?

I had also joined a therapy group that one of his associates, a clinical psychologist, led. I was a patient in the group, and in group therapy you do deep interactions with each other, and all the patients respond and work on each other in some ways, giving and sharing insights and feedback. After a few months, he pulled me aside, and said something like "You should go to grad school and get your PhD and become a psychologist. You already have the skills of PhD interns I have worked with, and you could do it."

Bill and Julie began saying the same thing. I was being bombarded by the same message: "Go into psychology. You are made for it." And internally the passion and interest were already there. I loved the study, and I loved the time I spent talking to people and processing together in these settings.

I began to pray as sign after sign just kept appearing. And then, I am not sure how to explain it, I felt as if God was saying "Go." It was an internal leading, prompting, nudging that would not go away. Finally, I said "Okay, God. I think you are calling me into this field. I surrender." I did not like the hard sciences, like biology and chemistry, so med school seemed like a long distraction into psychiatry instead of clinical psychology to do virtually the same thing. So, I was leaning toward a PhD instead of an MD.

Also, I was scared. I had two years of a business major behind me and was obviously way behind in amassing the prerequisites that would be required for a graduate school admission to a PhD program. Plus, the admission requirements were pretty tough for a PhD in clinical psychology acceptance. And then there was the reality of biting off five years of graduate school after college, an internship, plus another two years of supervised practice to qualify for licensure. It was sort of the equivalent of residency after internship. I would not be legit for another seven-plus years of training. Not to mention it was going to cost a lot of money. But I felt like God was saying "Go, and trust Me." I had to do it. There was no saying no.

So, in faith, I changed my major to psych, and enrolled in summer school to begin catching up with all of the prerequisites. A lot of work . . . but I loved it. I was alive. It felt like it was me. I was learning a truth that I later read in the Bible:

> ***A man's heart plans his way, but the Lord directs his steps.*** (Proverbs 16:9 NKJV)

My heart loved this path, but it took God to begin to direct my steps. And He did.

Over the next two years, person after person appeared out of nowhere and began to mentor me and offer me great opportunities for real-world experience. I had doors open to get pretty advanced training in psychodynamic therapy, Gestalt, Primal, ego psych, cognitive behavioral therapy, transactional analysis, object relations, and others. I was so fortunate to have so many mentors take an interest in me and teach me so much. It was inexplicable why they just "showed up" and offered so much help to me, but very experienced and well-known people, for no rational reason, began to offer to mentor me, as Dr. Minirth had. By the time I graduated from college, I had almost as much training in so many modalities as a third-year graduate student. And none of this was because I was very special or smarter than others in any way . . . it was all God opening doors to lead me in the path He wanted me to go. He was "directing my steps."

But by the end of college, I was also just wanting to be certain of pursuing this path. Strapping on all of those years of training to get a PhD seemed like a big gulp. I wanted to confirm the calling. So, I decided to take a gap year and work in a psychiatric hospital to see how it all really worked in real life. I had experienced all of that training, but only as a college student, not in real settings where I could be around real patients and see it all from the inside. It was all workshop and classroom experience, other than volunteering and assisting research in some residential treatment homes for kids. I needed to taste the real thing. Did I truly want to do this? I thought so, but I needed to be sure. But how in the world would I get a job with only a bachelor's degree that would really let me see the real work up close?

I prayed and searched. There were little things here and there, like group homes with the foster care system, but nothing truly clinical at my elementary level of education or experience. And then God intervened. Someone from the seminary suggested that I try to get a job as a psychiatric aide at the hospital where Dr. Minirth practiced. A psychiatric aide is a low-level staff member who works under the nursing staff, doing things like checking in on patients on suicide watch, delivering meal trays to the dining area, taking vital signs throughout the day, getting patients lined up for medications, sitting in on groups to follow up on patients' assignments, etc. Nothing that required training, but at least I would be on the floor and get to see the action. At the same time, it seemed like there was no way to get that job, especially at that hospital, where all of the seminary practicum students from Dr. Minirth's classes competed for positions, and other schools around Dallas. I was competing with graduate students. I didn't think I had a chance.

But it seemed like another step of "God might be leading," so I went to the hospital and applied. The nurse who interviewed me was cordial but discouraged me about there being any openings. I don't remember exactly how it happened, but somehow Minirth found out I was applying. A few days later, the head nurse called me and said that Dr. Minirth, no longer my doctor for a couple of years, had called her to recommend me for a psych aide position, and they wanted to hire me. I knew God had done it. There was just no other way. I had found a job.

But this was not without its obstacles. The pay was $3.33 an hour. I think that was minimum wage at that time. How was I going to live? But I was a bit of a scrapper, and I was willing to take a second job if I had to, and decided I would be able to deal with a year of poverty to get the experience. The pay was not the biggest obstacle; I could live cheaply to pursue my heart's calling. The big one was telling my father that I was a college graduate, from a great university, and I was going to work for three bucks an hour. I knew he would think I had squandered my education. While all my friends were headed off to big-paying prestigious jobs or going to law school or med school, or getting recruited by Fortune 500 companies, I was going to be almost starving with a college degree from a private university.

When I told him, he just shook his head. I could tell he thought I was nuts. And then when I told him it would be at least five more years before I could really even enter the profession, he just shook his head more. But then—and this is something I will always love him for—he just said, "Son, I don't get it. But . . . it's your life." He had to make it in life without an education, and he wanted my education to make it easier for me. I was seemingly throwing it all away.

I felt a bit of the same way that I had felt when I had to tell him I was quitting golf. He had been so proud of my competitive golf life, and I had let him down—or so I felt. Then, I had gone crazy to boot, and had to take a semester off of school to recover. And now this. I felt like a disappointing son.

But I knew something else at this point that would serve me for the rest of my life. He was not the father I had to please. I had a heavenly Father at this point that I was following, and this was the direction He was telling me to go. So, there it was. A tough moment for me, but I knew God was guiding me, and I had to take this step. He had opened the door, and I had to walk through it.

And I have to say, from that point on, Daddy was nothing but supportive. He was great. A little confused at my choices, but on my team. That's a good dad. And better than that, which was good for me, he didn't bail me out by paying for food or anything else I needed that next year. ☺ I had to figure it out, work a *lot*, and just trust God.

JUST OBEY

I went to work at the hospital and I won't chronicle all that I learned that year, but suffice it to say that it was clear God had brought me there. Although I was just an aide, the doctors began to bring me into their groups, and have me follow their patients through the days, helping implement treatment plans, and I worked closely with the nursing staff on the unit. The experience I was gaining was almost like being a psychiatric resident or intern. I was being allowed to do almost everything except official billable treatment and have patients of my own. But when you spend forty-plus hours a week in the milieu of a psych unit, you have a lot of interactions with the patients and the doctors. You learn their issues and treatment plans, and sit and talk throughout the day. They process everything they are doing in their sessions with the nursing staff, and the staff carries out a lot of what the docs are wanting to happen.

I was learning a lot about psychopharmacology, treatment, suicide, eating disorders, depression, and addictions. It was incredible as a learning curve . . . actually better in various ways than my doctoral internship after graduate training. And something else happened that would set me up for the biggest faith step yet . . . and another reason I know God is there.

Dr. Minirth and his partners who worked on that unit were using me for their groups a lot, sitting in the group therapy sessions. This was something all groups had . . . a member of the nursing staff was always in each group. But they were so gracious to me, always inviting me in theirs and sharing what they needed to make sure was happening with patients during the day. As the months of my gap year were passing by, they began to inquire about my graduate school plans. I was in the process of applying for PhD programs, and they got very interested in where I was thinking of going. I found out why one day.

They called me in and told me they wanted me to get my training somewhere close to Dallas, like Southwestern Medical School, or Baylor, because they wanted me to work for them and become a partner in their practice! I was shocked out of my mind.

They also said they could give me research work or other financial help to pay for school, and when I got through the master's level after two years, I could begin seeing patients with a marriage and family therapist license. I could not believe it . . . my future seemed to be secure and opening up before my eyes. I had "made it," it seemed. And I wouldn't have to move to Nashville for Vanderbilt or to Atlanta for Emory. I could keep my friends and community.

This was a dream come true. I was set. My life was lining up in front of me. So, I sent out additional applications for Baylor and Southwestern Medical School's PhD program in clinical psych, which both were nearby.

I had also sent an application to Biola University in Los Angeles, just because some of the best writing and research in the integration of psychology and theology was coming out of that school. It was the gold standard of that space in the field, and very clinically sophisticated. It was known for by far the best clinical training in the country in that niche. I had applied just for fun, really knowing there was no way in God's green earth that I was going to move to California. It might as well have been becoming a missionary in Africa. I was not even thinking about actually going. But it was a little like a kid applying to Harvard just to see if he could get in.

In February, I got a letter from Biola saying I had gotten past the first stage of applications and was granted an interview. They would send someone to Dallas to conduct interviews for applicants from that area of the country, and sent me an appointment time. I thought, *No reason to go to this, but what the heck, why not just do it for grins and to learn something.* It was on a day when a few friends and I were headed to New Mexico to go skiing, and I asked them if we could stop by DFW for an hour so I could do the interview. They laughed and said, "No! We have to get on the road, and you are not going to California anyway. Let's get moving."

For some reason unknown to me, I felt a strong prompting to go to the interview, so I told them I wanted to do it, and all they would have to do was give me an hour. They relented, with a lot of verbal abuse for slowing them down, and I went to meet with the interviewer.

The interview went well, and I liked the guy. We talked psychology, my future plans, and the like, and I found him to be pleasant, and the school's training to be impressive. We connected in a lot of ways about how we viewed psychology and faith. But I had no thoughts of anything past just the interview.

And then, it happened.

Something came over me . . . It was not like previous visitations from God where His Presence filled the room and changed the atmosphere. It was more internal, but definitely supernatural. My mind morphed. It was not like I changed my mind . . . it was like my mind was changed from the outside, yet felt "inside." It was a shift that I was almost an observer to. It was like my "being" was morphed into a certain awareness and almost command: I was going to Los Angeles. I was certain I had to go. It was a telepathic "knowing."

I have no idea how God did that, but I know it was Him. I walked out knowing I was supposed to go to California for my training.

I got into the car with my friends, and they sarcastically asked, "So . . . how did it go?"

"I am going to California," I said.

They laughed it off, and I repeated it. "I am going to California."

"Yeah, sure you are." They laughed. "You and all the other hippies."

We had quite a discussion, but my mind was made up, or made up for me, it felt. I was going to California for no rational reason that I could ascertain other than God had made it happen. It did not matter that I was leaving all of this great opportunity and professional security and valued friendships, community and other professional connections. I was to go to California . . . and it was settled.

As Proverbs 16:9 said, "the Lord directs his steps" (NKJV). I was being directed.

In August, I told Dr. Minirth and his partners that I was leaving, packed up my little Toyota with all my earthly belongings, no money to speak of, and took off. I was reminded of Abraham, whom God called out of his land to the Promised Land. In Hebrews 11:8–10, the author mentions that Abraham left Ur, not knowing where he was going, but he knew he was going to a city whose architect was God. I had no idea what I was doing, or what I was headed for, other than the architect of it all was God. All I could do was "trust."

I was learning a new truth in this spiritual journey:

> ***Trust in the Lord with all your heart and lean not on your own understanding; in all your ways submit to him, and he will make your paths straight.*** (Proverbs 3:5–6)

I had trusted Him before, and with all of the things He had done, this was no time to quit. I was headed for the unknown. What I had been learning and was to learn even more that has been true to this day, is that we can trust Him, even when we have no idea what He is doing. As the old hymn says, "Trust and obey, for there is no other way."

So, off to LA. And it was a big step of trust.

I'll never forget that drive from Vicksburg, Mississippi, to Los Angeles. It is a long way . . . much over the deserts of the western states. That means long intervals with not much happening. And that means long intervals of just being alone in my car, thinking.

What was I doing? I remember thinking a lot about how I was going to land in a faraway country literally not knowing anyone. No one. Not knowing where I would live, or who I would be around. Not much about what school would look like. All I knew was five years of "I have no idea."

But all the while, as I was asking those questions, I had an awareness of something that had grown in me: God will make a way. I just knew it somewhere inside, and now, decades later, I have found that to be a trustworthy statement. Sometimes the journey felt like following Moses through the desert . . . a lot of pain and feelings of being lost and going nowhere. But, over the course of it, as I have shared, He knew where He was taking me all the while. So, as I drove, scared in a lot of ways, I also felt a growing sense of anticipation of what He was going to do.

As I look back at this season of my life, I can see the collection of wildly creative and unexpected miracles God brought to my life to bring me to that time when I had gotten broken, to healing my depression, to finding my life's calling as a psychologist. He answered my prayer that first desperate day back in college in so many profound and life-changing ways that I was unable to recognize at the time as being the miraculous supernatural interventions that they were.

But they did not end there. After I had been healed up, and set on a new path, He then began doing many things to actually build the life I had been worrying about that fateful day way back in my dorm room. He put many things together after my arrival in LA, now knowing what lay ahead.

- He put me in a great community of further healing and spiritual growth when I got to LA. The people He surrounded me with were incredible. They felt "handpicked" for each aspect of my life that I needed them for.
- He gave me a family in LA who adopted me as their own, and continued the healing in me that Bill and Julie had begun, Guy and Christi Owen. They became my "home base" from which to build a life. They supported me and matured me in countless ways throughout my time in graduate school and beyond. They further healed me, and taught me how to one day have a family, be a husband and a father.
- He gave me the next round of mentors who trained me in incredible ways to prepare me for the work ahead of me, which I could not even foresee. I can look back and see that I was given several PhDs outside of the classroom by these shepherds He sent to me, as well as a lot of tenured and successful business mentors who taught me how to build businesses. He schooled me way past school through the people who adopted me and took me under their wing.

- He led me to specialized healers who got to the deepest aspects of the injuries and traumas and immaturity that I was not yet finished with, as there were many unhealed parts of me as well as a lot of growing up to do.
- He placed me in the perfect first job, which would direct my path for decades to come, giving me my first business partner, who taught me the ropes I would need to set up a professional practice, clinically and organizationally, as well as introducing me to the field of leadership.
- He gave me a business mentor at twenty-five, who taught me almost everything I know about business, who remains in my life today.
- He placed me in a new field of organizational consulting work, where I was kind of forced to begin developing models of psychological and spiritual growth that spawned content for a later publishing path I had never envisioned.
- He led me to expand my interest in psychology from just the clinical world to the world of leadership consulting, and then supernaturally called me into it with a repeated almost audible voice when it was time to make the shift.
- He put me in a prayer relationship that led me to launching a hospital system, where content would be honed and developed for decades to come.
- He dropped the first hospital deal in my lap when I was unable to make it work, which led to building a company that had hospital units and treatment centers in forty markets in the western United States.
- He literally pushed me into media, which I was terrified to do, and that led to a nationally syndicated radio show for almost twenty years.

- He pushed me into television media that landed me on major networks as an expert commentator and contributor.
- He literally cornered me through a group intervention into writing my first book, which I was totally ill-equipped to do, and assigned someone to the task of making me get it done, which launched a publishing career, which somehow at this point has released over forty books with around 20 million copies sold.
- He healed my inability to have a successful relationship and led me to the best wife and life partner I could have ever had.
- From our relationship, he gave me two daughters, who are the light of my life.
- He gave me my ability to play golf again competitively, healing my wrist after He had redirected my life, and I have enjoyed it for decades since, and it has brought many incredible relationships and much community into my life.
- He continued to give me incredible friends and community and mentors who have supported me, healed me, corrected me, modeled for me how to be better, and given my life the deepest meaning I could ever have hoped for.
- And, in some ways this should be at the top of the list, Moses said that God has given us His statutes, his "ways" that would preserve our lives and lead to real "thriving" that is lasting, way past the things I had once thought would bring me happiness. He has taught me and taught me and still is teaching me those principles and they have changed me and the entire way I do life. I would have been lost without His "ways."
- Plus, He created German Shepherds and Dobermans . . . to make me laugh, enlarge my heart, and give me more

joy than I can count (okay, maybe not a "miracle," but I do believe He made them for us to love and enjoy ☺).

God is an active worker of miracles, both in the mundane corners of our lives and in big, bold ways that literally move mountains. Some of the above may seem "circumstantial," but the impossible odds and ways that those developed which were totally outside of my orchestrating is miraculous to me. And in the next section, I will get more into the truly supernatural events I have experienced.

At this point, I will end the blow-by-blow steps of my journey to finding faith. This book is not meant to be a life memoir. But, next, I do want to share with you a few more stories about other miracles in my life for one purpose: so you can see how real and alive He is and how dependable He is to be with us in life. And while I am sharing with you some of the great things He has done for me in my life, I'd like to ask you to remember that the entire list above of good things that God has brought about, just like the Moses story through the desert, was also riddled with a lot of pain, struggle, defeat, failure and the like, as I have said. So, don't think a journey with God, like mine, is all a bed of roses. And please don't think that all of those good outcomes, happy endings, in life listed above came in any way because of some great ability I brought to the table, or heroic performances on my part. Quite the contrary, God has been able to bring about all of those blessings in spite of my weaknesses, immaturity, flakiness, character flaws, and many foibles. *I have gotten in His way more than I have helped Him get me to a better place in life than where I was in that dorm room.* The harsh, and beautiful, reality is that He is the One who has done it all, with a very broken person, as I have openly shared as best I know how. He did it just like He promised me in the worst of my brokenness that first day with that verse, and He has done it in spite of having to do it with this broken, fractured, incompetent human. As He said, He came "to seek and to save that which was lost" (Luke 19:10 NKJV). My life was lost, and He found me and put it back together. And I share that for anyone who might be reading this to give you hope that no matter where you find yourself, there really is hope that life can get better. And if you are not "lost in life," but have not entered into having faith, or are struggling in faith in some way, I share it to show you that He is very real and can be trusted, even when it looks like anything but.

So, this really is a God story. It is my testimony, like the blind man He healed one day who had been blind from birth, and all he could tell the other people who asked about it was "I just don't know about all of that . . . All I know is that I was blind and now I can see . . . and this man Jesus did it" (paraphrased from John 9:25). That is how I feel . . . all I can tell you is that I was a mess, and He has done a lot to make it better. And, the message to you from me is this: He wants to be in and work miracles in your life too. Whether you are stuck like I was, or doing "great," He has a plan for you that is better than you will ever know.

Part II

How I Came to Believe in Miracles

The Bible depicts a life that can seem contradictory, and confusing. Yet one of the things that helps me know the Bible is true is that it talks about life the way it really is. It depicts life exactly as we see it. First it says that God will be with us, bless us in various ways, protect us, lead us, and guide us. I have shared a lot about the truth of that as I have experienced it. And at the same time, on the same pages, it says that horrible things might happen to us as well. Death, loss, disease, betrayal, poverty—these are all horrible things that it says He allows. It is such a contradictory message. But it is exactly true to the life we see, even after we begin to follow Him. There is good and bad, both in the Bible and in real life.

I always say that God has a marketing issue. Brands always try to paint a totally positive picture of what they are selling. "Come with us and you will lose two hundred pounds. You will get rich. You will look like this . . . People will fall in love with you. You can break par after five swings . . . etc." You never hear marketers talk about the downside except when the FDA makes drug companies list all the possible side effects in a commercial. Everywhere else, it is usually all positive. (By the way, shouldn't the doctors do that instead of a commercial?)

And in God's marketing, He does promise us a lot of good stuff . . . Jesus said to follow Him in order to have an "abundant" life. I like that. He promises to "bless" us, whatever that might mean in various contexts. But He *also* promised us suffering in life, and even extra suffering if we follow Him. Not only from others, but the suffering of self-denial, having to give up some selfish and unloving patterns and the like. Suffering sometimes when we "love our enemies." Not exactly a great marketing approach: "Buy this product, and you will get to carry your cross daily! Buy a life with Me and it will cost you big time." Yet, He does tell us the truth. Most products say if you use it well, you will live a long life and be happy and successful. But the only one who ever did it perfectly in God's storyline got crucified. And so did many of His followers. Not what they teach you in marketing school to be honest about those kinds of outcomes if you buy their product. But that is what He does. He tells us like it is. That helps me have confidence in the Bible . . . it does not try to make it all look rosy. It mirrors real life as we find it. God is not afraid of reality.

As I was remembering some of the examples I wanted to share with you where God showed up and did miracles for me, so many stories came to mind that served as examples of the promises of God's abundant life, plus the pain that goes with it, and then the goodness of God showing up in the trouble. But that is what makes suffering with God different from suffering without Him—when we suffer with Him, we do not suffer alone, and as I have shared, He is with us, and because of that, the suffering is very different. As the Bible says about going through losses of loved ones, when we know Him, we "do not grieve like the rest of mankind, who have no hope. For we believe that Jesus died and rose again, and so we believe that God will bring with Jesus those who have fallen asleep in him" (1 Thessalonians 4:13–14). In other words, we know that death is not the end of our relationships or even our own lives. We can be back together with loved ones again. So, even suffering through losing people we love has a different flavor to it when we have a relationship with Him.

So, in sharing a few more experiences of "God showing up" in my life, I hope you enjoy these short anecdotes that show only a handful of the many interventions into life that I have seen God perform. These experiences have helped build my faith and I hope they do that for you as well.

The following stories reveal a very important reason why I believe. Throughout my journey of faith, I have found out something important: God does things. In pain and suffering, and in times of "normal life." Some of them are dramatic, and some less so. But in each one, I was able to clearly know it was Him who was showing up. As they say sometimes, "you can't make this stuff up."

The Naked Pastor

It was a horrible day, one that directed and limited my life for many years after, and was the source of a lot of pain.

I was in the seventh or eighth grade, and it was the day for oral book reports. I usually liked that day, as enjoyed hearing everyone and also sharing in front of the group myself. I liked public speaking. So, nothing new.

But for some reason, this time, about a third of the way into it, I got flustered. I began stammering and stuttering, and it got worse. I could not recover for some reason, and found it hard to go on. I just got further and further kind of unable to get the words out. Kinda paralyzed in front of the room.

Then the teacher stood up and said, "Just sit down. This is terrible," or something pretty close to that. She then went on to kind of berate me with things like "You will never be able to be a success in anything if you can't do public speaking. And you can forget ever being a lawyer [one of my possible career dreams at that time], because lawyers have to talk in front of people."

Needless to say, I was devastated. Ashamed and dejected, I just slithered into my seat and tried to disappear.

From there, it went downhill as far as public speaking was concerned. I had no trouble with a few friends, like at a table or something. But any time the group got to be any size at all, I just literally could not speak. Not "wouldn't," but "couldn't." So, I didn't.

I went all the way through high school and college avoiding any kind of public speaking at all. I would always refuse it. Even asking questions in class became a real difficult thing to do and hide my problem, so I rarely even did that. In high school, my parents sent me to a counselor to cure the problem, but it did not help. And to make sure you understand, it was not just a fear. It was "I literally can't do it." Period. I couldn't talk. In fact, it was so bad that I almost flunked twelfth grade English, because there was an oral book report requirement and I was ready to tell the teacher "Well, flunk me." And I had been recruited to play college golf . . . ready to lose it all because of my inability to go through with it. In graduate school, I pretty much continued to avoid any public speaking, other than in class for a question or a small discussion.

So, roll the clock forward to my mid to later twenties. I had been in practice for a few years and was building a lot of models of psychological and leadership growth and working with companies and organizations. As a result of all of that activity, I was continually being asked to speak for the organizations, businesses, churches, and the like. And . . . I always refused. One hundred percent.

When asked, I would just say, "No, that's just not something I do." And let it go. No way was I ever going to stand in front of a group again. I went about my private clinical and consulting practice, and that was enough fun for me. Small meetings around a table were okay, but nothing larger.

Then one day, I was at the gym and headed to the showers when this big naked guy walked up to me. He was huge. (Actually he had played NFL football for the LA Rams.) I was wondering what he wanted when he looked at me and asked, "Are you a Christian?"

That seemed weird . . . big naked guy randomly walking up to me asking if I am a Christian.

"Uh . . . yeah," I answered.

"Well, God just told me to tell you something," he said.

My first thought was "Well, I am also a psychologist, and I can make those voices go away." But I didn't say that. I just replied, "What?"

"Yes, that's right. Don't worry, I am not a weirdo. I am a pastor. And God just clearly spoke to me about you," he explained. He then told me he was a pastor at the Newport Vineyard Church, a good place that I was familiar with. So I agreed to talk to him.

We went next door to a restaurant and sat down, and this is what he said: "God said that when you were a kid, something bad happened to you that has made you afraid to speak in front of people ever since. But He wants you to begin speaking for Him, and He is going to open some doors. You are to walk through them."

I was *stunned*. How in the . . . ? *What?* That was all I could muster. We talked some more before I left there and went to my office. I just sat there literally in shock, amazed at how *real* and present God is all the time. And once again, how long I had suffered with that problem . . . and yet He had been there all along. Aware, loving me, but doing nothing about it.

Until now.

In high school, when I was struggling with it, I prayed a lot for God to help me, and He never did. But now, it seemed like He was stepping up. There was no way I could deny what had just happened. That naked guy did not know me from Adam, nor what I did, nor anything about my problem or where it had come from.

The next week or so, I got two calls to speak to public groups. ("He is going to open some doors for you to speak and you are to walk through them.") The first one was a Presbyterian pastor gathering with about fifty pastors. That would have been far more than I would have agreed to and been able to do. But this time, I literally felt like I had no choice. Zero chance that I was not going to do it, no matter how scared I was. God had entered my space and told me to do it . . . and I could not run and hide. I was afraid I would get swallowed by a whale if I did. I was way more afraid of how real and alive He was than whatever could happen if I melted down speaking.

So, I asked a good friend of mine who prays for me, and also is a speech therapist, to come with me for support. She sat on the front row, and I stumbled my way through it. Barely. I don't remember if they even liked it or not, but at least I had gotten through the first test without passing out.

From there, it was more and more practice as more "doors" began to mysteriously appear, out of nowhere. I was petrified each and every time, but gradually, I got more and more comfortable. It took about a year or so to feel more comfortable. Then, I was offered a radio show and was suddenly talking to a *lot* of people. Before then, there would have been no way.

That was decades ago . . . since then I have spoken thousands of times. And now, I actually enjoy it, and though I sometimes get a little helpful dose of "butterflies" before going up, I do not have any *fear* of going up. God has healed that, this time through showing up through a naked pastor and telling me to do it, and then a natural process psychologists call "desensitization" and "exposure." It is the gradual facing into what you fear, and the brain slowly learns that the seventh grade teacher is no longer there. In fact, as I write this, I just came back from speaking at a global leadership event that had hundreds of thousands of live attendees in arenas and auditoriums all over the world. And it was actually fun. As a psychologist, I believe the slow healing came through natural processes. But there is no doubt in my mind that the impetus to get me into that process was supernatural. How else can you explain it?

My stepping into it would never have happened without a supernatural intervention by God through a naked pastor who did not know me from Adam. Who knows where and how He is going to speak, but what I have learned is that He does.

God as GPS

It was the end of the day, and I was in my office after seeing patients when my pager went off. I called my answering service, and they patched me through to a woman on the phone, calling from a phone booth. I knew who she was, a new patient I had seen for only a couple of weeks, but she was pretty depressed. I had discussed with her the possibility of a hospital if the depression got worse. She had resisted.

"Hey," I said. "What's happening?"

"Nothing," she said . . . in what I could tell was a voice that did not sound good. "But I wanted to call you and thank you for trying to help me. I know you want to . . . but I just can't do this. I just can't. So, thank you anyway."

And she hung up.

I was afraid—in fact, I knew—what that meant. She had said she was not planning on killing herself and had promised me she would call me if she ever felt that way. But I knew at that moment something had happened and she had changed and made a decision. She was going to do it.

And I had no idea where she was, how to get help to her, or find her. This was before cell phones. I called her home, but no one was there. I was totally in the dark, and very scared.

When I feel scared, I pray. So I did. I asked God to keep her safe. There was nothing else I could do. Until . . .

I felt a prompting to go get in my car and look for her. But it made no sense . . . I had no idea where she was. Southern California is a big place, and I would not know where to begin. But I followed the urge. I went to my car.

I felt a nudge from somewhere to drive to South Coast Plaza, a very large shopping center in Costa Mesa, California, about fifteen minutes away. I truly do not remember why . . . if it just came to mind or I felt a leading from God, or I had wondered maybe she was shopping there . . . I don't remember. I had no idea whether or not she would be there. What I do know is that there was no way to find her, even if that was right. It is massive. It has over 250 stores and what seems like miles of parking lots and streets in many directions. Even if she was there, how would I find her? The entrances are on several streets and different blocks. No way to know where to begin.

But I began driving. When I got to the general area where turnoffs start and there are various parking lot options (think almost like Disneyland), I would just feel guided to the next turn. A nudge to turn here and then there. Different lots in the complex and rows and rows of cars. Each stop would be like that, not knowing what to do other than getting an internal nudge to go this way or that, exactly like the day years before when God led me to the pastor. I just kept following the "prompts," having no idea where I was going, until . . .

I turned down a row of cars and there it was: her car. I recognized it from seeing her in our parking lot. It was hers for sure.

I drove up to it, and didn't see anyone in it. I got out, and there she was, lying down in the back seat, staring into space, pretty detached. She had her pills and was ready to take them. Tragedy averted. God had saved her.

The story has a good ending. This was years ago, and she fully recovered and thrived after a lot of therapy. She had three children after that and a great marriage to a good guy. The chances of my knowing where to go and being able to drive right to her car right in time apart from God? In my mind, zero.

He Protects

One example in my life where I followed God into a promise, and then experienced a lot of pain, and then found Him to be present in the pain was when I began our psychiatric hospital company. I had been seeking God for the next season of work for me . . . I had been in private practice for about six years but was having some stirring in my soul that I wanted to do something different as well, and something more. I had a friend who was in the same season in his life as I was, so we committed to getting together every Thursday evening to pray about our lives and next steps. We did this for about a year, every week, when it became very clear that God was calling me to begin a faith-based hospital. I had no doubt. It was a very exciting time in my life, along with Dr. John Townsend, who built the chain of treatment centers with me, to see it all come together and see the incredible team we had that was healing and changing lives. But this fulfilling calling from God was not without struggle.

Besides the difficulties involved in a startup business, I quickly discovered that when you begin stepping into gnarly family situations on a large scale, you invite trouble. I had dealt with difficult families and abuse scenarios before in private practice, but hospital work took it to a different level. Situations that require hospitalization often involve abuse, both spousal and sometimes child . . . and often extended family conflict that is so ugly it is staggering . . . I had to get over my shock more than once. (The Bible is not kidding when it says that some people do really evil things, and warns us to not be surprised, but I often am.) When you help a woman escape spousal abuse, for example, sometimes the husband will come after the ones who helped her. Sometimes when you help a depressed adult escape ongoing abuse and control from an extended family, they will attack you.

I don't remember the specifics of the particular cases we were dealing with, but I remember clearly what God did for me. There were a few really tough ones at that time when we had patients who had been admitted for treatment, and were setting some boundaries with the abusers, and the family did not like it . . . at all. In some cases their churches didn't like it, either, so they were coming after us. From attorneys and legal threats to people trying to go to the press to write untrue, slanderous articles and use various other tactics, they were fighting us as they lost control of the people they were abusing.

And as I said, surprisingly, not only families but some were Christian groups and churches that didn't like psychologists or psychiatry. They thought we were on the wrong side . . . turning people away from God. They wrote articles and books about how bad our teachings were and how we were heretics. One church group, for example, broke in the hospital through the ER in the middle of the night in literal special ops clothing with hoods, like a religious militia, to "rescue" one of their church members who had admitted herself for depression and an eating disorder. In their minds, they had lost control of her to us—the "secular humanists"—who were turning her from God. In reality, we were helping her escape a very sick religious system and giving her *back to God*. But they were on the attack. Little did they know there was a police station two doors down and a very attuned nursing staff.

It was in a season of what felt like a lot of that was happening, and I never had experienced anything like that before in my little private practice. This was a war I had not ever had to fight, and honestly, the first time doing it was a bit unsettling. (I'm used to it now. ☺) I knew we were helping people and doing the right thing, but the attacks were getting to be gross and very distracting from how we wanted to be spending our time. I felt a bit victimized at times, like "Hey . . . I am just trying to help here. Why are you attacking me??"

One night I was particularly distressed over all of this, worried about the threats, had been praying about it, and then it happened. I can't remember the event, but I was somewhere and someone came up to me and said that he had had a vision about me. He said something like "God showed me that He has a wall of protection surrounding you, like a wall of fire, protecting your 'house' . . . with angels, protecting what seemed like it is your 'house.' But the 'house' wasn't really a house . . . it seemed like it might be your place of work, but it is kind of like a 'house.' And the specific protection is around protecting you from people's family members who are attacking you in some way in that work."

And then he pulled out a piece of paper where he had drawn what he had seen with the "wall of fire" protecting the "house." There was no doubt that the house was the hospital, my place of work, where people lived for a little while like a house . . . a home. He was protecting the work that we were doing from those who did not like it. The drawing showed that we were being shielded by God. And we continued to be, with no threats ever materializing into anything of consequence. Even one time when a man called and said he was coming to kill Dr. Townsend. The police were able to find him, a man who had just been released from prison for attempted murder of a police officer, and arrest him before anything happened.

It was another example of how He is with us, even when things are hard. And a supernatural vision from a stranger brought security to me, in the midst of all of that going on around me.

God's Provision

One of the consistent themes of the Bible is that God will lead us into a new season, vision, or calling . . . and we have no clue what it might look like. Beginning with Moses calling His children to the Promised Land when they had no idea what that was or how they would get there, to Abraham being called out of his homeland of Ur and "not knowing where he was going," as the Bible says in Hebrews 11:8 (NKJV). Then you have Jesus just walking up to virtual strangers, saying "follow me," and they do it. They know the call is real but have no idea how it will all come together.

Rarely do they have VC funding to begin the new venture . . . he just provides manna for the day. (That was the food that God provided to the Israelites when they were in the desert trying to get to the Promised Land. He only gave them enough for each day, so they would learn to trust Him.) The journey with God very often involves His telling us to do something, and our not knowing how it will come together until He provides. And that provision, very often, comes *way* after we would like it to.

I shared with you how I took my first step like that when I left the security of everything in Dallas to follow God to LA. And he provided. About six years later, again I found myself in a secure place with life going pretty well . . . until He began to stir and develop a vision inside me to begin a psychiatric hospital that was faith based and "faith friendly."

At the time, psych hospitals and psych units were very different from today, in a number of ways. The most glaring one was that, back then, you actually had enough time to treat people well and accomplish a lot with depression, severe anxiety disorders that were debilitating, eating disorders, bipolar illness, addictions, and the like. Up to thirty to sixty days at times. You could go deep with them, and, if needed, with their families as well. And notice that most of those maladies are illnesses you probably know well because you have friends or loved ones who have suffered with them. As you know, they are pretty normal people, who would have really benefitted from a month of intensive treatment in a hospital where getting better was all that they focused on.

But, today, chances are they never get that opportunity for longer inpatient treatment because the insurance industry has changed so much that treatment centers like that barely exist anymore. Today, the insurance model is often more geared to denying treatment, and instead only medicating and stabilizing the patient, and getting them out of the hospital as soon as possible. They only usually pay for really severe kinds of cases, just to protect and stabilize quickly. Unless you have private funds to go somewhere pretty expensive and pay for it yourself, your chances of getting thirty days of inpatient treatment are way slimmer than they were back then. Now, there are way fewer options. It's sad.

But when I started out, that kind of treatment was readily available, and you could do a *lot* with someone and their family in thirty days or even more. It was so incredible what could be accomplished. But there was often one problem for people of faith who wanted their faith to be a part of their healing and therapy . . . since many hospitals and the ones in charge saw a lot of religious abuse, fixation, and ideation, there was a lot of bias against it. Often, when someone checked in, their Bibles were taken away, and they were probably not going to find a prayer group happening on the unit. It was often not "faith-friendly." But I had come from Dallas from a faith-friendly psych unit run by Christian doctors and had seen the benefit of patients' faith being understood and, more than that, being a part of their treatment and healing journey. Not long after, the APA grew a specific division dedicated to faith and the spiritual aspects of psychology. And that is what I clearly heard God telling me to go do: start a faith-based hospital treatment program.

Knowing that faith was not welcome in many hospitals, and knowing that psychologists were limited by the medical establishment at that time as to what they were allowed to do in hospital settings (we could treat, but had to admit a patient under a psychiatrist, for example), I knew that my vision for what I wanted to do as a psychologist would be limited by the powers that be in the medical establishment. They had control . . . that was a bummer.

So, I figured out a way. If I couldn't control what goes on in the psychiatric unit as a psychologist, how could I get control? Wait . . . I could control it if I owned the hospital, right? Good idea, I thought. I decided to buy a hospital. (When you are in your late twenties, you haven't learned how hard some things are to do, what the heck.)

I had no money of that magnitude . . . buying a hospital would take millions that I did not have. I was just a young psychologist in my twenties starting out. But I did know that the old saying "it takes money to make money" was not true.

Most entrepreneurs start out with nothing, and I certainly fit that description well. What is true reads more like this: "It takes money, but it does not have to be *your* money. It can be someone else's money." All it really takes is that you have something of value and then other people will bring their money to join what you have that has value. Value brings money. I thought my idea had value, and I could provide a valuable treatment program, so I figured out I could find money that would invest in that value. Armed with that belief, I set out to find the money.

And I did.

I found the investor who would put up the money, and since I knew nothing about actually running a hospital (which is very complicated with regulatory issues, insurance issues, nursing unions, etc.), I also went out and recruited a hospital administrator to join us. Now, all we had to do was buy a hospital, and I could have full control of what happens in treatment. I could find psychiatrists and psychologists who integrated faith into their work, understood it in the patients, and pastors and churches who would come alongside us and help bring mental health services to an underserved population consisting of people of faith. We were off and running.

Sort of . . . but soon, not at all.

We found some hospitals, all right . . . and we made offers, but no one would sell. They were doing too well at that time. We could not get a deal, nor could we start a new one, either, because California had a "certificate of need" law that prevented new hospitals from being started. So, my vision was seemingly dead. Not going to happen.

But I knew God had called me to do this . . . I just knew it. And I also knew I just couldn't do it in a partial way in a hospital where I did not have control, for I would be blocked every time I wanted to teach a group about how faith can help with your mental health issues, or have a prayer meeting, or have chaplains working on the unit I was stymied. After two years of working on this . . . my vision seemed dead in the water. But my prayer partner and I continued to pray.

Then it happened.

I was sitting at home watching golf on TV, and the phone rang. It was Dr. Frank Minirth, calling out of the blue, from Dallas. I had not talked to him in probably five years.

"Hey! How are you, and what are you up to?" he began.

"OMG! Hey, Frank! So good to hear from you!" I said.

"So, what are you doing these days?" he asked.

"Funny you should ask," I said. "I have been trying to start a hospital."

"Really? How is it going?" he asked.

"Well . . . I'm stuck. I literally have everything in place. I have the money, the network of pastors and churches for support, media relationships for marketing, some great psychologists and psychiatrists . . . and . . . no hospital. I cannot find a facility. I am all dressed up and nowhere to go. No hospital," I bemoaned.

The phone was silent for a bit . . . and then Frank said, "Well . . . I have a hospital in LA and nothing else. We should talk."

Oh my gosh . . . could this have been true? I was dead stymied in my vision from God that I knew was true and real, yet it felt like He was not providing. Nothing was working. Until He did. I now might have a hospital, and I would have control! I knew Frank would align with what I wanted to do. The vision was coming true! And Frank had no idea what I was up to, and for some reason, after five years, he calls with exactly what I needed.

I flew back to Dallas within days and we joined forces. We made a deal.

So, we formed a new company to do this one hospital, and I could have control of all the treatment, and Dr. Minirth would provide the facility through a relationship they had with a national hospital chain who gave us carte blanche. I was off and running.

Then, God dropped another piece of manna from heaven. Dr. Minirth had a syndicated radio show in the Midwestern and Southern United States, and said they would bring their show to the LA market, and that could help us with marketing. People could find out about the Christian treatment through the daily call-in show, and that would really help us.

When I realized that we were going to now have a significant media presence, I knew that this could go much faster and be bigger than I had first thought, and I wanted help to do it. Someone I could trust and respect, and I knew who that was.

Dr. John Townsend and I had been doing work together, thinking about faith and treatment models for a while, and had taught some workshops and had done radio together as well. And besides respecting his thinking, he was one of the best clinicians I knew. And one of my closest friends (my best man at my wedding). We would have a blast. He was the only one I would have trusted with this.

So, I returned to Newport Beach, where I lived then, from Dallas, and asked him to join me. We were off and running. Much more to the story, as God provided many, many more rescues that we needed at just the right times, too long to chronicle here. Just one quick example though: . . . It took us about ten months to get everything in place. The advertising materials were done, the team was on board, and we were a few weeks from opening. And then, I woke up one morning and read the business section of the paper, and there it was . . . the hospital company we were working with had entered chapter 11 bankruptcy! And they had never told us! Dead in the water again . . . no hospital. They were shutting down weeks before we were to open.

God? What are you doing?

We prayed, and we hit the streets, knocking on doors. We realized from the previous hospital partnership that we did not have to own the hospital, as had been my original vision. We just had to have a deal directly with the owners where they would give us control of the entire psych service, and then we can still do what we want to do. The medical establishment would work for *us*. All the owners care about is that it works.

Right in the nick of time . . . God led us to a hospital that was owned by two older doctors who had retired, and they liked us. I think they got a kick out of seeing these kids who wanted to do something different, and they were intrigued by the faith aspect. So, for some reason, they said okay. They even threw in a fully furnished medical office suite for our outpatient service for free, since we were broke. Once again . . . He had a plan all along and was taking me step by step. Even when I thought things were hopeless.

We got to help a lot of people, and that one Los Angeles radio station turned into the largest Christian radio network in America. They took our show to their new stations as the network grew, and as they did, we opened up more hospital units and treatment centers. Eventually, we had treatment in over forty markets in the Western US. John and I directed that company for over a decade and eventually through a merger, the radio show was syndicated on over two hundred stations nationwide. And one of the things I am most gratified by was that our faith-based treatment was researched by outside university researchers and found to get superior results compared to industry standards across several diagnostic categories of mental health. We were able to present those findings at the American Psychological Association's national convention.

All of this came from a God who leads, and where He leads, He provides what we need at each step. Not without struggle, pain, or crises, but with faithfulness in the midst of all of it. It was one more lesson of trusting Him. I instantly knew that random call from Frank was no coincidence at all.

Reunion with Jesus

I love boats, and I have loved them since I was a little kid in the bathtub. From there to fishing, duck hunting, alligator watching, and water-skiing, I was hooked. I carried that love into adulthood, and as soon as I was able, I moved into oceangoing vessels. I love deep sea fishing, going to islands anywhere, and scuba diving. And when Tori and I started dating, she instantly fell in love with it, too. It is a love we have shared over decades now.

For years, we had a boat anchored in Newport Harbor and were on it quite a bit. One night, we had spent the night on the boat, and when we woke up the next morning, a boat had pulled in the slip next to us during the night we had never seen before. It was really an interesting beautiful older boat . . . and had actually just returned from Hawaii, where it was in a movie being filmed there. It was a beautiful classic old trawler.

I was admiring it when the owners came out on the deck, and we started talking. We heard a little more about their story, and they seemed really fun and interesting. Since we were spending a lot of time redoing the interior of our boat, we were down at the slip a lot, and gradually got to be friends with them. Soon, while we were having dinner one night, they shared the real reason they were there.

Nick had pancreatic cancer. He was a successful tech entrepreneur who had cashed out of his company at fifty, and he and Kaitlin had just begun their adventure of traveling the world when he got the news. As he shared, it did not look good, with a very low survival rate. They had come to Orange County to see an oncologist there who specialized in this type of cancer and were going to live on their boat for a while. We were so sad to hear their story . . . right in the prime of life with so much to look forward to, and now it looked bleak.

As the weeks went on, Nick and I got to be good friends. We shared an obvious passion for boats, and for business, and red wine. And he was funny and fun. I liked spending time with him and hearing about his business story. He had written some code years ago that turned into a very big product. The journey sounded like a good novel. I loved hearing it.

In the process, I had shared my story, too, and he knew I had a faith-based chain of hospitals and treatment centers, and had written some books on faith and psychology. One day, he opened up.

"So, I need to talk to you about something," he said. "About God."

"Sure . . . what is it?" I asked . . . wondering what had prompted this.

"Well, I have told you that I converted to Judaism from growing up Presbyterian, right?" he asked.

"Yes, you did," I replied. "You said that the idea of a Trinity did not make sense to you, that it seemed like three Gods, and you believed in one God."

"Right . . . and I still do. But the problem is that I do not hear of a lot of Jews praying or believing in healing . . . only the Christians do. And I know you are one, and I wanted you to pray for me," he said. "I need healing."

"Of course . . ." I said. "I would love to, and I also would love to hear more about your faith story."

So I prayed for him and had others praying for him as well. I loved Nick . . . I didn't want him to die.

And there was another backstory happening as well. Kaitlin, it turned out, was a believer in Jesus. One night she pulled me aside after dinner and asked me if I would talk to Nick more about faith in Jesus. She wanted eternal life for him . . . as she was really afraid of what was looking like a soon-to-come end of his life on earth. She wanted the assurance that he would be in heaven.

We talked about it a little more, and I found out more about his journey. I began to bring the topic up with Nick, and we had some good beginning discussions. A lot was about the bad experiences he had had growing up in the church . . . a story that I have heard many times, which causes many who grew up around Christianity to leave the faith after they get out of their house. His was no different. For him, though, as he was a spiritual person underneath it all, converting to Judaism gave him a place for his faith without the baggage he had grown up with. I admired a certain spiritual tenacity he had. I empathized with how he had been treated. (More about that topic in a later chapter.)

But, sadly, soon after we had begun these talks, Nick began sliding downhill. He lost a lot of weight and had no strength. He was dying, and conversations were becoming too painful, both physically and just not having the strength to engage. It was sad to watch and to walk through with Kaitlin, as we had grown to love her, too.

One Saturday morning, my phone rang. It was Kaitlin.

"You have to come down to the boat . . . Nick is going to die today. I am sure of it. You have to come," she said almost frantically. I knew she was worried about his dying without knowing Jesus. I said we would be there.

When Tori and I got to the boat, she met us in the main salon and said he was in bed down in the master stateroom. I went to see him. He was kind of propped up, and registered a tiny smile, about all he could muster. And his eyes showed that he was happy to see his pal.

I said a few things, and then I said, "Nick, can I talk to you about God for a little?"

He nodded, and it was apparent that it was a really engaged nod. You could tell he wanted to hear whatever it was.

I said something like the following: "So, you know how you told me that you grew up in a Presbyterian church where you just could not put together some of your experiences with a faith that made any sense?

He nodded.

"Well, as you know, I understand that . . . in fact, a lot of what my work is about is helping people recover from bad treatment by churches and religious leaders or religious people, or even goofy beliefs. So, I get that for sure. I understand how that turned you off. I was glad that it made sense to you now, as an adult, that those people and their behavior do not necessarily negate Jesus, and you understand that not all Christians are like they were . . . at least, you have agreed to hang out with me!"

We smiled.

"And you also talked a lot about how the idea of the Trinity, of God being one God in three persons, just didn't make sense to you, and it seemed like that was a big issue for you, so you converted to Judaism. And that is what I want to talk about . . . Okay?"

He nodded.

"I believe in the Jewish God also, the God of your Scriptures. The God of Abraham, Isaac, and Jacob. That *is* the Christian God. But a lot of Jews don't know how their own Scriptures point to Jesus, and prophesy of the coming Messiah and specifically how they would know *who* to look for. Because the truth is that Jesus fulfilled every one of those prophecies. *Every* one. But there is one I want to talk about now that you know well. Remember when you were learning the Jewish faith, and learning about the Passover?"

He nodded.

"Remember how there was a lamb that was to be sacrificed, and then the blood of the lamb was to be put on the doorpost of every Israelite's doorway? And then the angel of death, who brought death to the Egyptians, would 'pass over' that house and everyone would live? Exodus 12:13 [NKJV] says 'When I see the blood, I will pass over you,' and the blood of the lamb would save you?"

He nodded.

"Well, Jesus *is* that Passover Lamb, the Messiah who was prophesied to come. He was the perfect Lamb of God who was sacrificed to pay the death penalty for all of us, and it is by His death and resurrection that we are forgiven.

"Jesus lived a perfect, sinless life and so He was the fulfillment of the entire Law of God. Being perfect, He was the only one who could pay the penalty of our imperfection. So, He sacrificed himself, and He died and was raised from the dead to prove who He was. And He promised that when we put our faith in Him, the 'Passover' that He became applies to us. God forgives us as a result of our faith in Jesus.

"We are forgiven all our sins and are made right with God through faith in Him. We know that His claims of being One with the Father are true because they were proven by His resurrection. He proved He was God.

"So, I am *with* you in your Jewish faith. I believe the same things about God you do, and your faith, our faith, says that there would be a Messiah to come, and Jesus was that Messiah. He *is* that Messiah.

"So . . . this is what I want to ask you . . . Would you like to receive Him as your Passover Lamb now? And go to be with Him as He promised?"

Nick looked up and nodded . . . yes.

I said, "Okay, just repeat this prayer after me . . . even if you can't say it out loud, just in your heart: Jesus, I believe in you as my Lord, and I believe that you died for my sins and were raised from the dead. Please forgive me for all of my sins. I receive you as my Lord and my Savior."

I watched as he followed along . . . and then tears began to stream down his face. I knew that he had returned home . . . he had found the God that people had driven him away from with their bad and hypocritical behavior. He was now at peace with God. His face was different. I looked at him and cried with him. Then, I kissed his forehead and said, "It's okay now, Nick. I know you need rest. I will go now, and thank you for talking to me."

He nodded and smiled, squeezed my hand while still teary, and I left.

As I walked up the stairs, Kaitlin looked at me, and I nodded a big yes. She knew what that meant and ran down the stairs to the stateroom.

I went up to the salon and told Tori what had happened. We just sat there until we heard a painful scream. We ran downstairs, and Kaitlin was convulsively sobbing over Nick's body. He was gone. After a little bit, with our help, she came upstairs and collapsed on the floor, sobbing. Months of pain and agony had now broken loose . . . all the times she had to be strong were now releasing, as she fell into the pain she had carried. She was overwhelmed with grief.

Tori was kneeling over her as she sobbed on her knees and face in the floor, with her arms around her. She was sobbing and sobbing, with Tori just comforting her. I went over to the counter in the salon to get some Kleenex, and then it happened.

I looked up from the galley across the salon where Tori was kneeling over Kaitlin as Kaitlin sobbed . . .

And standing next to them was Jesus, and Nick.

I saw them. I do not have any way to describe how I know they were there or what it was like, other than I know they were. It was not like an open vision, as I have heard people describe. Not like a movie screen. Nor was it like seeing two people standing in the room with my real eyes in a real visual field. It was almost like they were translucent . . . and I was "seeing" them in another dimension. Like I did not even see them with my eyes but in my spirit, inside, somehow, even though I saw them kind of visually as they were standing across the room. Every time I have ever tried to describe this moment, I fall short. I cannot describe it.

All I know is that I know they were there, standing over Kaitlin while she wailed in her grief. They just stood there next to her . . . just watching her. Like "being with her" in some way, but not doing or saying anything. They just watched. They just stood for a few moments, or a minute. I'm not sure. It was just a moment of their being there with her.

Then—and this is what blew my mind—*they instantly "flew" up and to the left through the ceiling and wall, and up into the sky.* Gone. Instantly gone into the clouds. Up and to the left is the only way I know to say it, through the ceiling and the wall at warp speed. So fast.

I was stunned.

I have doubted and questioned this so many times because it seems so "out there," but each time I come back to the truth I know . . . I saw it. Otherwise, where did it come from? It wasn't a thought. I think stuff all the time. It was not a picture in my head, like all of us can picture things at any moment. It was something different, on another plane, one I have not seen before or since. And I know it was them.

To close this story, I have to also tell you what Kaitlin told us later, when she stopped crying. She said after Nick and I had talked and she knew that he had connected with Jesus, she talked to him a little about them, and her love for him and then she said she told him, "Nick . . . I know what happened with Henry. And it's okay now . . . You don't have to hold on anymore. You can go."

When she said that, she said he looked up at her into her eyes and nodded. And then she said something happened she could not believe. All of a sudden, he bolted with a face full of awareness and what she described as a look of "amazement." He looked upward with eyes wide as they opened fully . . . and he was looking up at something . . . something above him that had really surprised him and caught his full attention. His face lit up, she said, with something she described as like a "total realization" of something and like he was overwhelmed with whatever he was seeing in another dimension. Then . . . he was gone.

I know that he saw Jesus . . . his newly found Jewish Messiah, who had come to receive him and take him home. And he probably saw a lot more as he was looking past this dimension into the next one. I am glad that he had the Good Shepherd coming to take him home.

God's Perfect Shrink for Me

Most people I know didn't marry their prom date. Usually, unless you live in a country with arranged marriages, we all can relate to some period of traveling through and negotiating the world of "dating." It can be a lot of fun (I loved it) and/or a fair amount of brain damage (had some of that too). Also, my belief is that it can be an incredible context for personal growth and learning. Sometimes, and more often than not, that growth is ushered in by failure or heartache.

That was where I was. I was in my midtwenties and by that time had dated a lot, and dated some really, really great women. For the most part, I didn't choose a lot of crazies . . . at least any that I hung around with for very long (although some of the nuttier ones were really fun). I was fortunate enough to like some good women and was lucky enough to choose well. And that ultimately was what revealed my problem.

I could see that I had a pattern. There were women who were really, really wonderful people, that I liked, was attracted to, and had good relationships with. Until . . . for some reason, and no good reason, I would slowly begin to feel depressed. Interest would wane, and I would feel like it is just not the right relationship. So, I would leave. What was the most painful was when I knew there was nothing really wrong with them, but the closer I got, the more depressed I would get. So bad that I just couldn't stay in it. I would just shut down.

As part of psychology training, we were required to have individual therapy. I had been with a really good therapist who had helped me immensely in a lot of areas of life. But after one more failed relationship, he finally said to me out of the blue, "I think you need to see a woman therapist for this issue. There is something I am not getting to that you need to work through, and I think you need a woman to do that with."

"But Phil . . . you are the best. Why can't you do it?" I said. I really liked working with him.

And this I think was the "God" moment:

He said, "I don't know . . . it is just a feeling I get. You need a woman therapist."

Little did I know that God was about to change my life again.

"So, who would I see?" I asked. I knew all of the good therapists around there, and I could not imagine who would be better or who I would like to see, or trying to find one that I didn't know already.

"Well, I heard that Althea Horner just moved from New York to LA. Why don't you call her?" he said.

"Yeah, right . . . like why don't I call Jack Nicklaus and ask him for a golf lesson? Why in the world would she take my call?"

At the time, and in the overall history of psychodynamic therapy and psychoanalytic thought, Althea was one of the two or three most heralded names in the field. She wrote the textbooks we had all studied, and she lectured all over the world. She was more than famous and, I was sure, unreachable, especially for a beginning psychologist. Like a kid with a garage band calling Bono and saying "Come write some music with me."

"I don't know," he said. "Just a feeling. Why don't you try?" (Another God moment.)

I left that day with my head spinning, mainly because Phil wanted me to change. I had been with him for a while, and it was going to be a loss. But the idea did kind of track with me . . . maybe I did need a woman therapist. I *was* having issues with committing to a woman.

I went home and thought about it more. Althea? *The* Althea? I had heard her speak at a training conference once, and she was so high up on such a pedestal. To listen to her knowledge base was mesmerizing. No way could I even get to her, and who knew if the rumor that she had moved to LA was true anyway. And if I met her, I think I would have been too starstruck to even speak. Plus, why would she even agree to see a beginning therapist like me?

How could I find her? There was no internet then, no way to google her. What the heck . . . I dialed 411, directory assistance, on a lark.

"Directory assistance. May I help you?"

"Uh, I need a number."

"What city?"

"Uh . . . I think probably Beverly Hills . . . West LA maybe?"

"What name?"

I gulped and said, "Dr. Althea Horner."

"Hold for the number . . ."

And then a recording spit out a phone number. Seriously? She is here? Is that even the right one?

So, I dialed the number for what I figured was her office and a wall of gatekeepers, preparing to somehow make my feeble request.

"Hello?" a woman's voice answered.

"Uh . . . yes, I am calling for Dr. Horner," I said.

"Yes . . . this is she," the voice said.

OMG . . . can this be happening? It was really her? She answered the phone???

I told her I had heard she had moved to LA and I was a psychologist just beginning and had a training therapist but was looking for a new one and wondered if she might see me. I can't tell you how feeble that request probably sounded, as I was waiting for her to laugh.

"Well, I just moved here and haven't really set up a practice yet . . . but this sounds interesting. Why don't you come in and let's talk about it," she said.

What???

"Uh . . . sure. When?"

"Well, I am moving into my new office still, and tomorrow is a holiday, so I was planning on being there setting up, so could you come then?" she said.

Of course, I went, and for some reason, she agreed to work with me.

This was in the summer, and we went through the early phases of her getting to know me and all of that. We talked about my dating history and all the usual stuff. Nothing earth-shattering about the first few months of therapy. Later, in the fall, I developed a hernia and had to go in for surgery. It was scheduled for a few days ahead, and as it was approaching, I began to have weird anxiety symptoms, almost panic type feelings, which was strange for me. I had had a few surgeries by then in my life and no fear whatsoever. In fact, I kind of liked it because the pre-op Demerol shot was so amazing. ☺

I went in for my session and told her about my anxiety over the surgery. She asked about my experience in hospitals with doctors . . . and I told her about my childhood illness being in a wheelchair and braces for all that time, and about how hard it was for me and my family. (See earlier chapter.) She asked how I got better, and I told her that there was a woman doctor who saved my leg from amputation and how we would drive four hours one way every week for a couple of years to see her, and how she really saved my life. She had become as powerful a figure to me as my own mother. My whole world revolved around her for a couple of years. I really loved her.

"Wow . . . she played a really important role in your life," she said. "Do you still see her?"

"No," I said.

"Why not? Seems like you would at least keep in touch after all of that . . ." she remarked.

"She died," I said.

"Oh no . . . when? How?" she asked.

"She was murdered . . . right as I was finishing treatment with her," I answered.

What happened next still sends chills down my spine.

Althea's face turned white . . . she looked shocked. She leaned forward in her chair and said, "Her name was Mary Sherman."

Now I was the one who was shocked.

"Yes . . . how did you know that?" I asked.

"She was my best friend," Althea said.

She then told me how they had been together in training, and had been really close friends until her death. And what happened from there brought the healing I needed for my "inability to commit" problem.

Althea brought in pictures of Dr. Sherman, and told me stories about her, and was able to recreate her in front of me enough to help me recall her and remember her. More and more memories surfaced as she made her real again. Through that, finally, all of the grief over losing this powerful second mother began to come out. I began to melt, and feel everything I had never felt about losing Dr. Sherman, my second mother.

Looking back, it made sense why I had never grieved. I will never understand this, but the way I found out she had died was that my mother just said it to me in passing one day, and then just dropped it. And we never talked about it. I am not sure why, but that is how she handled it. Maybe it was too hard for her to tell me and talk about it, but she walked into my room and just told me. She walked out, and that was it, is all I recall.

As I worked through that grief, it became clear why I would begin to get depressed and bail out of a good relationship as it got closer. Getting close in a relationship, feeling a deeper connection, would activate the loss that still lived in my soul, depressing me, and I would push away to avoid another loss if I got closer and made a commitment. The unconscious fear of loss can make people do very self-destructive things, like leave perfectly good relationships. "If I love you, or need you, you will leave me. So, I'll leave you first."

Althea helped me discover that loss, recreate Mary Sherman, and grieve her, which healed that dynamic in my life. It is the reason I was later able to find the most incredible woman in my life and make a commitment to her with no fear at all. As of this writing, Tori and I have been married twenty-eight years, thanks to Althea. I never once got depressed or had fear after Tori and I met.

I am so thankful to Althea; she was an incredible woman. I will always be grateful to her.

But it is also a thanks to God for His healing me through her. I had been praying about that dynamic and pattern in me for a while . . . seeking answers and could not find them. Begging God to make a relationship work. But He knew how to heal me. He mysteriously led me, through Phil's hunch, to the *one therapist in the entire world who could have recreated Dr. Sherman for me and healed me in that way*. What are the chances I would end up with Dr. Sherman's best friend as my therapist at just the time I needed that to heal me? It takes a lot of faith to believe that was a coincidence. More faith than I have. ☺

My Biggest Miracle

I have shared some of my dating drama from my single years . . . it wouldn't even make for a crummy romcom, so only one more. But those years did include some God moments along the way as you've seen. He entered into the pain, and healed me of what was holding me back. But, I still had to find her . . . the one.

I thought I had, a few times after that. As most singles know, there are relationships that you think have potential, and then some that you think have real potential. Right after the breakup with a particular woman I thought had real possibilities, I was really discouraged about ever finding the "right one." It was a bad night. I was in my room, and pretty disappointed with God . . . I had felt like this one was going somewhere, and then it didn't, and I thought He had let me down, since I had thought He was the one who brought us together (which He probably did, to learn something, anyway).

And to really set the stage for this miracle, my dating life then had developed a theme to it as well. There would be some great girls who had wonderful character and values, but the chemistry or whatever that "magic" is would be missing. Not unusual an occurrence for singles dating, but disappointing at times when you wish there was more in this relationship because they were such good people. You like a lot about them, but there is a spark missing. Then there were women who I really liked and connected with more chemistry, but either spiritual depth or our values were not the same and I knew they were not for me. Almost any single person probably knows that feeling as well . . . relationships where there is something on either side of the equation just missing. I had not succeeded in finding the one who had "both." One who was more of the "all" that I was looking for. I was once again disappointed, because this time it had seemed as if both sides were potentially there. Yet, she decided to move on.

I was talking to Him about this problem in my room one night, and felt a very strong "go open your Bible" prompting. If you don't have a relationship with God, that might sound weird. But if you have for a long time, you know what that feels like when it happens. Sure, sometimes it could just be indigestion . . . or nothing at all, but this time I was pretty sure it was Him.

So picked up my Bible and just opened it, and the same thing happened again that had happened that day in my dorm room, years before. It "randomly" fell open to a page in the Old Testament, in the same way, and this verse jumped into view:

> *We are witnesses! May the Lord make this woman who is coming into your home like Rachel and Leah, from whom all the nation of Israel descended! May you prosper in Ephrathah and be famous in Bethlehem. And may the Lord give you descendants by this young woman who will be like those of our ancestor Perez, the son of Tamar and Judah.* (Ruth 4:11–12 NLT)

Wait . . . a woman is coming into my home? Really? Seriously? This is what *really* got me, and I *knew* God was speaking to me: *She would be like Rachel and Leah. Both of them.* If you don't know the story, Jacob had been very attracted to Rachel (the magic and chemistry) and secured her for marriage from her father, Laban, and then Laban tricked him into taking both of his daughters. Jacob had to work for seven years to get what he thought would be Rachel as a wife, and then after Laban tossed Leah into the deal, he had to continue to work to pay it all off. And there was no magic with Leah, no chemistry, yet she was the one who developed the great character. Rachel and Leah represented the two kinds of women I kept finding, never able to find both of them in one person. Chemistry and character.

Be all of that as it may, and the other vicissitudes of the story, what hit me was that the woman who was "coming into my home" was going to be *both*. One like Jacob was in love with, and the other whose story was one of developing great character and devotion to God. Rachel was the one he was smitten with from first sight, and as was revealed over time, Leah ended up being honored about her character and devotion to God, for which she was given favor.

What I knew God was saying was that He was going to bring someone to me who would be everything I had longed for. Someone I would be in love with who also had all the values and depth that I cared about.

I knew that He had spoken to me. I knew it.

What I did *not* get was that there was more to that passage than I was connecting with. I just kind of ignored and didn't notice the "seven years" part of it that Jacob had to wait.

Well, the years went on. I continued to date and had some good relationships, but no Rachel and no Leah. I thought I had misunderstood. Then, one night at a Christmas party, a friend brought a guest whom I started talking to and, after a while, was very interested in. We talked for a couple of hours, and I was going to ask her out, but then she said something about just being in town to visit her family. And she said something else that made me wonder how old she was. I was in my early thirties. And I had thought she was about twenty-six or twenty-seven, as she was mature and had a lot of life experience. But slowly it became apparent from some things she said that she was in her early twenties. That just seemed too young, so I passed. Plus, she did not even live where I lived. It would be a long-distance relationship with someone way too young.

But I did not forget her. It was like she stayed somewhere in my head, but it felt different. She wasn't in my mind thinking about her as much as like she sat over to the side, if you will, in my spirit or something. Just present somewhere in my head and soul. She remained and every now and then, I would think of her. Kind of camping out somewhere in my head, even though I had only met her once. She never left.

Roll the clock forward almost a year later, and I went to a party to see a friend's band play, and there she was. It turned out the party was for her sister and she had come to Southern California just for a day or two to attend. Totally random . . . but there she was. We visited again and the same kind of connection happened. But, she lived across the country at that point, and still, seemed young in the math of it all. So, again, I didn't pursue.

About five months later, I was at a business dinner and walked through the bar and I saw her sitting with a friend of hers. I couldn't believe it . . . there she was again . . . a random occurrence again in a populated region (Southern California) of over 20 million people. Strange . . . she didn't even live in Southern California.

I went over and said hi and they asked me to sit down, and this time we talked for another two hours. The same weird feeling was there again . . . but again, she lived across the country and was only in town for a couple of days. Just visiting again. Too far, and too young, I said to myself. So, I passed again. But, I could not forget her, even more after this meeting.

And this time, something hit me. I started to think about it, and it felt like she was hanging out in my spiritual awareness somehow. She wasn't just in my head. It seemed like God was putting her there. Can't explain it, but that's how it felt. So, I called a friend of mine who prays for me and had been through a lot of my dating sagas and told her about it. I said, "Look, there is no way I am going to pursue this . . . she is too young, and she lives far away. But it feels like this is way too random, and it feels like a 'God thing' to me, possibly. And since there is too much complication, I am not going to do anything, but if it is from God, I am going to ask Him to do something to show me, and I want you to begin praying about it. I am not going to look for her or pursue her [which was unusual for me in my dating life]. But if this is from Him, I want you to ask Him to do the impossible, since she lives across the country. Ask Him to arrange another 'random' meeting as a sign, and if that happens, I will ask her out." My friend said she would pray, and I left it at that. Although she did not leave my head.

Roll the clock forward. Four months later, I attended a graduation ceremony at a high school for a friend's son. Just another ordinary day. I went up to the punch bowl, and someone spoke to me. I turned around and it was her mother, whom I had "randomly" met at a party the week before. She said "hi," and then she said, "You know, Tori's in town. You should call her."

I was shocked . . . here it was. A random open door. And why in the world her mother said that, none of us know to this day.

I immediately called a few older friends of mine who had daughters in their twenties and asked them how they would feel if a guy in his thirties started dating their daughter. All of them said, "That's no big deal. If he is a good guy, I wouldn't think twice." That was all I needed . . . even though it still was nothing I had done before, dating someone in a different decade of life.

I got her number and called her and asked her if she would want to go out, and she said, "Actually, I would." So, we did. I'll never forget that call or that answer. It was like she surprised herself by saying yes.

Well, the date was horrible. She seemed different. Nice and cordial . . . but just kind of distant and cool. I went home bummed . . . I thought this was going to be something, but I didn't see it that night at all.

But I started to think . . . *I know God is in this. I am going to try one more time.* Even though at this time, she still lived across the country and hadn't aged any more than I had. The gap was still there. But after all of this, I just couldn't let it go.

I called her again about a week later. When I offered a night, she said she was busy that night. I would offer another one, and she said, "No, I am busy that night too." I offered another one, and she hemmed and hawed a bit and said she had plans that night as well. Finally, I said, "Okay, how about tomorrow?" As it turns out, her doorbell was ringing and she was rushed, so she quickly said, "Okay, fine," just to get me off the phone.

I found out later that she had the same issues with the age difference as I did, and that was why she had been so aloof and chilly. But this time, she just said yes to get me off her case as the doorbell was ringing.

We went out the next night, our second date, and something happened. We had a great time. Those issues kind of vanished somehow, and it was really good. We went out again the next day, and then continued spending time together over the next couple of weeks. Mind you . . . she was only planning to be in town for a little while, attending a two-week art institute . . . but . . . we were having a great time, so she decided to stick around longer. Longer turned into longer, and here we still are, twenty-eight years later.

My biggest gift from God.

Do Not Sign It

It was at a point in my publishing career where things had taken off, and it was "free agent" time. Like in sports, when you are not tied down to a team anymore, you are free to sign with anyone. In publishing, after finishing a contract, it can be a fun and exciting time as well. All the publishers are coming around wanting to do the next book or books, and it is a fun time to get together with them and think about next projects.

All of the season of meetings was over, we had finally reached an agreement, and a good one for several reasons. It was for several books and would give me a clear path for about five years. I liked having a direction set so I could just get to work on writing. We had finalized the negotiations and would be signing in a few days.

I was at home after dinner talking with Tori, and my phone rang. It was a woman with whom I served on a board and only saw a couple of times a year. I knew her, but not that well, and she was certainly not current on anything I was up to or working on. She knew nothing about my work with publishers.

"Hey, Shelly. How are you?" I asked.

"I'm good," she said. "But I just had a vision about you."

"What?" I asked. "Really? Tell me." This was not a normal occurrence for me. I was pretty new to the world of people having visions at that time.

"Well, it was very clear. I saw you in a yard, and you were talking to people in the yard, and there was a fence around all of you. Like a fenced-in yard. And then the Lord said this: 'You have been speaking to people in the yard, and he wants to remove the fence so you can speak to people outside the yard.' And, he says that you are about to sign some contract . . . I think it is about a book project or something . . . and he says if you sign it, it will keep you in that yard. So don't sign it."

Oh my . . . I was so certain things were going so well and my immediate future had so much clarity. And now this . . .

"So, Shelly . . . Are you sure? . . . This is from Him?" I always tend to ask that when I get people who have "messages from God." There are a lot of kooks out there, and I rarely believe them. But this one . . . this had too much credibility in both the message and the messenger. It was so specific . . . and I knew exactly what it meant, too.

The deal was with a Christian publisher. And no matter what the title or subject of a book, if the publisher is Christian, retailers often will tend to bury it in the religious section of the bookstores (which actually existed at that time, before Amazon and online book buying). And the marketing would be mostly to the Christian world . . . and that what that meant was clear in the vision: *the* people in the yard. God was telling me that He wanted me to talk to people outside the Christian world, outside the yard, and He was going to move the fence. How in the world would she know that I was (a) about to sign a book deal, and (b) one that would keep me talking to a certain closed group?

Another reason I also knew that this was real was that for about a year and a half, when I would go out on my patio to pray, I would hear a voice in my head say, *I am taking you out of the ministry.* That is all it said, and it was clear. But I did not know what all that meant, other than for me, it did mean something very specific. I was supposed to begin working outside the "Christian" world of audiences that I was speaking and writing to. To me, at that point, "ministry" meant Christian audiences, which, back then, was most of what I did. And what I would discover soon was the message from that voice also meant much more about my publishing, leadership consulting work, business speaking, and media.

"Yes, I am sure," she said. "It was from God. It was clear."

I hung up bummed. Everything had looked so good, and now I knew I had to walk away from so much that was secure. But, as I learned way back in leaving Dallas, when God says "Go," you do it, and you leave security behind. He will provide the next place to land. So, I walked from the deal.

I won't bore you with the details, but the publisher was dumbfounded and could not believe we were not going through with it. It made no sense . . . unless you were on that phone call. And then, it was confirmed.

Soon thereafter, Time Life called with an offer to do a book with a national secular media campaign they were doing with a music offering that would take the message way, way past the Christian audience I had been speaking to up to that point. So, John Townsend and I wrote a book for them called *God Will Make a Way*, and the beginning of talking to people outside the yard had begun. Now that the "fence" was beginning to be removed.

But there was much more to come. And this was the real fulfillment of the next stage of the vision. Now that I was free to publish "outside the yard," God (through some other God-directed clear steps, some "random" circumstances), put me with an outside-the-yard publishing agent who wanted to do my first secular business book and take it to a New York publisher, which would full-blown be outside the yard. And I would be writing to businesses without the Christian language in the book, which would mean that they could now use the principles in their public companies and secular businesses. I had always worked in the secular business world, doing leadership consulting, but all of my books up to that point had Christian content in them, and most companies didn't want to offend people with that and would not use my books. This step was fulfilling the voice I heard on my patio about God taking me outside the Christian world, as well as the vision about talking to people "outside the yard." It was all coming true, exactly like both the voice and the vision had said.

We went to New York, signed a deal, and published a leadership book that showed the principles that I had been using with leaders for a long time but had no Bible verses in it to scare people off. Cleanly outside the yard. (It is weird . . . if you say "It is good to be honest" in a book, people love it and think you are smart. But if you say "The Bible says it is good to be honest," you get canceled, and they think you are "one of those" religious kooks. So, I didn't use any Bible verses in the book at all; I just shared the business leadership principles that I use in the companies I work with. And at various times, they would lead to some great conversations about why I believe.)

Well, things happened, as the vision had said. The *New York Times* reviewed the book (it was called *Integrity*) and called it "the best book of the bunch" in the leadership books they were reviewing. That turned it into the launch of a new direction for my writing and a new audience . . . the secular business world. Although I had done CEO coaching and leadership consulting for twenty years at that point with many secular and public companies and had built and run my own businesses, my brand in publishing had always been pigeonholed in the Christian yard. God took me out of that for His reasons and supernaturally directed me to do it through the vision and the "voice" I heard. Had he not, I would still be "in the yard, and I would have missed so many great opportunities to meet and work with so many people who don't hang out in that yard, for purposes that were His.

He does guide us . . . even when we think we know what we want to do. He closes some doors that we desperately desire, for other reasons we might not understand. Just like I thought I wanted to follow my golf dreams or continue down my publishing track as is had been unfolding, God wanted something different and better. Again, the proverb rang true:

> *Trust in the Lord with all your heart and lean not on your own understanding; in all your ways submit to him, and he will make your paths straight. (Proverbs 3:5–6)*

Kneecap

I had landed in Phoenix and was checking into my hotel, getting ready to speak in a few hours. The gathering was Jewish rabbis who believe in Jesus as the Jewish Messiah. (It always surprises me how many people say, "Really? I didn't know that was a thing . . . Jews who believe in Jesus?" They often do not know that Jesus was a Jew and that the entire faith of the New Testament is Jewish and authored by Jews. But that is another topic we will touch in an upcoming section on how Jewish prophecies proved the Messiah to me.)

I was really excited to be speaking there, because since I was a little kid, and today, so many of my friends have been Jewish, and I always relish hearing about their traditions, families, values. I always feel at home with my Jewish friends and colleagues. I felt like I was "coming home" speaking there.

I walked into my hotel room to unpack, and it happened. I saw a very clear internal vision or picture in my head of a kneecap. Very clear. And I heard the word "kneecap" go through my head. Not an audible voice, but an internal one . . . kind of like a loud audible thought, if that is a thing.

I thought, *What the heck?* I didn't know what it was. Then it happened again, and kept happening. I knew it was not coming from me, and just wondered if God was saying something to me. And it kept repeating: *Kneecap. Kneecap. Kneecap. Kneecap.* I had no idea what to do other than pray, asking God to show me what this was about . . . if it was even Him. I thought I might be imagining it . . . sort of. But not really, because it was just too clear and strong. I just had no idea what it was about.

So, unable to fully shake the feeling of it all, I went down to the ballroom where the five hundred or so rabbis were gathered. I sat in the audience for a little bit while the session was opening and heard nothing about a kneecap from the stage or in my head. Maybe it has passed.

I got up on the stage and began to speak. My talk was going pretty well and rather normally when it happened again, as I was speaking. *Kneecap. Kneecap. Kneecap.* My head was getting a bit crowded with that word bouncing around and the picture interrupting me. What was I to do?

The short answer is that I had no clue. So I just kept speaking and made it through the noise in my head to the end. No one noticed that the psychologist was hearing voices, and nothing dramatic happened that night. No one offered me medication or a straitjacket. I just mingled a little with attendees and then went to my room.

When I got there, I was still hearing the repetitive *kneecap* every once in a while, and I just began to ask God what He was trying to tell me. I got nothing back.

The next morning, I spoke in the morning session, and it was more of the same. I gave my talk, and inside my head I was hearing *kneecap*. Every once in a while I would see the picture in my head, too. Still confused, I kept speaking, finished, went back to my room, prayed, and got no further in understanding.

So, on to the final talk that evening. The awareness of *kneecap* was still front and center, and this time, I knew I had to do something about it. It was too real to ignore. So, at the end of my talk, wrapping it up, I said this to the audience: "I am not one of those preacher types who goes on TV and says things like this . . . in fact, I am not a preacher at all. But I have to share something with you. I feel like there is someone here who might have something going on with their kneecap and need prayer for it. So, I am going to pray for you right now, and if that is you, please come talk to me when we are done."

I then prayed from the stage for God to help whoever it was who had a kneecap issue and to heal it.

I left the stage and went to the back of the room to the audio control table to deliver my microphone when a woman came up to me, all excited.

"That was me you prayed for!" she said.

"Really?" I asked.

"Yes," she said. "I have been having an issue with my knee and a lot of pain."

"Wait . . ." I said. "Your knee?"

"Yes," she said. "My ACL was torn, and I have had a lot of pain."

"Oh . . ." I said. "I am so sorry. It is not you. I am looking for a kneecap."

"But . . ." she said, kind of surprised.

"I will pray for you," I said, "but I don't think I was talking about you. I was talking about someone with a kneecap problem." I prayed, and she walked away . . . I don't think all that happy.

I continued with the audio guys, and then a tall Middle Eastern man walked up to me and said, "I am the one with the knee you were praying for."

"Is it your knee? Or your kneecap?" I asked, having already had one miscue.

"My kneecap. I have had an infection under my kneecap for a while and the doctors cannot figure it out, and the pain is unbearable at times. Sometimes the pain is so bad, I cannot even go to the office. I really needed to be here because of my work, and I didn't think I could make it. But I did, and I have been in a lot of pain.

"Okay . . . it is you. Come with me to the greenroom," I said.

We walked across the hallway and went into the greenroom, but as we were entering, the ACL lady returned and wanted to come with us for more prayer. I had to scoot away quickly to get to privacy with the right guy, all the while feeling bad for her.

I closed the door behind him and said, "Okay, I want to pray for you."

He looked up at me and said, "No . . . you don't understand. I was sitting in the audience when you were speaking and was in a lot of pain. I was crying out to God silently to please help me. Then, you prayed . . . and when you did, I felt a bolt of electricity go through my entire body, and it was like my knee caught on fire."

"I am healed," he exclaimed.

He then rolled up his pants leg, pulled off a knee brace, and threw it across the room.

I was stunned . . . I had certainly had not expected that to happen as a result of the noise I had in my head the evening before! But it was another example of when God is there and we have no idea how true that is.

I can safely call that one a miracle.

A Helping Hand

I love the practice of clinical psychology. I love the science, the study, the content. It captured me in college when I began to read it. More than that, though, I love feeling the gratitude of being able to play a part in relieving someone's suffering . . . I guess, at my core, I am a "healer" more than anything else, as others in helping professions can relate to. Call me codependent if you will . . . but I just like helping people. Occasionally it has gotten me into trouble in giving "too much," through working too much, but mostly it has been really gratifying at deep levels. And past the painful cases, I also really love seeing people just "get better," even if they are already a high performer, like a CEO or professional athlete who is already thriving but wants to go from "good to great." I love seeing people thrive . . . taking the next step and winning.

But it is not all roses. Psychologists suffer along with their patients. As Freud said, "No one who, like me, conjures up the most evil of those half-tamed demons that inhabit the human breast, and seeks to wrestle with them, can expect to come through the struggle unscathed."[1] How true. It can be a painful profession as well as fulfilling and gratifying. Some research has shown that practicing psychologists die sooner than those in other fields. Sharing pain and fighting dysfunction can take its toll.

Most of the difficulty comes not from difficult patients (like malignant narcissists, for example, or when you get physically attacked. I have left more than a few sessions bloodied and bruised). The real pain comes from seeing the suffering and hearing the evil that has been inflicted on some people. Just hearing their stories. Sometimes I have left the session and vomited after hearing what happened to someone. Some people's abuse is unimaginable. So, walking the path with people can be painful as well as fulfilling. All helping professions can attest to that.

But the other pain psychologists experience from time to time is, for me, the hardest: pure powerlessness. It is the feeling of "I just don't know what to do now to help. Nothing I am doing right now is making this better." At times you feel like you have done all you know to do . . . you want to end the pain, and you can't. At least not in that moment. How many times I wished I could avoid hospitalizing someone, but at that moment, it was the only option until more progress could be made.

That is why, many times, I have been so grateful that I was not doing this alone. God was there and many times intervened. Recall the earlier story about the suicidal woman he led me to finding her in her car, just in time. Here is another one of those examples that absolutely startled me when it happened.

I was treating a physician who was a highly accomplished woman. But, secret to all but a few, she also suffered from severe PTSD from being raped as a little girl. It did not emerge or even hit her until she was in her early thirties and out of her residency. She got severely depressed and then began to have some dissociative episodes, like you see sometimes in dissociative identity disorder (in the old nomenclature, "multiple personalities").

Fortunately, she was not dissociating in her professional life, as the dissociative states came only at moments when she was triggered in some personal way. At least at this point, she was still able to work. Her kind of practice was not stressful, and in fact kind of protected her. Thankfully also, she was single with no immediate family conflict and lived with a very understanding roommate, and the triggering could be contained when it happened. It mostly occurred when seeing something on television that was violent, seeing a show or movie where a child was hurt, or after a phone call with her family of origin. I would not even let her talk to her father. I did not want her working either, at least for a while until we could know the triggering risks better, but she adamantly refused. She was not a danger to anyone, so there was not much I could do. She was so determined to be an overcomer that I could not even keep her from watching TV shows or movies that might trigger an episode.

On this day, in my office, as she was talking about the abuse with me, she hit a memory that put her over the edge. She flipped into what seemed like a four-year-old girl, totally with the voice, gestures, and expressions. I had seen this before in other patients who had suffered severe, severe abuse, and usually knew how to deal with it, having worked in this arena a lot before her.

But this day was different. As she was talking about it, she went from screaming and reliving the abuse to connecting with me as I was trying to pull her out of it, and then she totally "switched" in a way I had not seen her do. She had seemed to be headed back to her "normal adult," I thought, flowing back from the childhood dissociative state. But when she turned into an adult, it was not her normal self at all. Instead, it was a steely, hard, and almost viciously determined adversary toward me. *Viciously* angry with contempt. She said, "I am going to kill myself, and you can't stop me. I will not do this . . . I can't. I won't. Leave me alone! Leave me alone!" With that, she got up and headed for the door. This was a personality I had not yet met.

I could not let her go, as I knew she was serious and not in her right mind. She *would* kill herself. I got in between her and the door and stopped her, not easily, and suddenly she went still and slumped over. Collapsed. Totally unconscious. Nonresponsive and catatonic. I sat her down and tried to get any kind of response from her. I even checked her pulse, as it looked like she had suffered a heart attack and died right there.

She had a pulse and was breathing but totally unconscious. I tried everything to bring her out of it. But this was certainly one of those moments of powerlessness on my end. I did not know what to do. I was about to call 911 to hospitalize her, but I stopped for a moment, since she was safe in her dissociative state, I felt, and her vitals were normal. I wondered if there was some way to reach her, bring her back, and avoid putting her through the trauma of emergency services and involuntary hospitalization. I began praying. I laid my hands on her head and prayed for God to help in some way. "God, bring her back somehow" was about all I knew to say. "Help me."

Suddenly, she kind of quickened, showing some aliveness, but clearly still in another state. This was after several minutes of my trying to get a response and getting nothing. Then, still in some altered state, she said, "Who is that? Who are you?" staring off somewhere in the distance . . . then silence, as if she was looking at someone else, not me. I was totally irrelevant as I tried to talk to her. She was unaware of me, but very aware of someone else I could not see. She kept her gaze fixed on "someone" I could not see. I had no clue who it was, or where in her head this person lived.

Then she said, "What a nice white Light . . . such a nice light . . . he's so nice . . ." Then she began nodding and seemed to morph into a very different state . . . and totally relaxed. And she began talking to the "light." Soon, she began nodding to the light, saying . . . "Okay. Okay." In some way, she was communicating with someone I could not see.

After a minute she came to and looked at me, almost looking befuddled, like she didn't know where she was for a moment. I sure shared her befuddlement.

And then she said this, with a look of bewilderment: "A white light came to me and just stood there and surrounded me . . . and I felt safe. And then, he told me, 'Listen to Henry. He will help you. Do what he says. It will be okay. But you have to listen to Henry.'"

She paused, and then she said, "It was Jesus."

And she was back to her normal state. One hundred percent sane and would pass any mental status exam. And she was totally aligned with me and the process again. Still having a *lot* to work through for sure, as we continued to work for quite a while until the PTSD was gone. But after that moment, she was on a very different path with a very different kind of hope. Ultimately, she was successful in resolving the depression and the PTSD, accomplishing much professionally as well. And my powerlessness was relieved . . . for another day.

Now, I know some psychologists might say that was just some sort of connection she had with an internal introject (a fancy word for people we have internalized inside our heads), or a more benign alter. But I have never seen that happen like that, and I have worked with many, many dissociative episodes. In my view, and also in my clinical understanding of her in particular . . . I know different. It happened the very moment I prayed desperately for her (and I was praying in silence). He came to her. And it was different from any state she had ever been in or was in after that day.

In many other tough moments in her life as she continued her recovery, she would recall that moment and lean on it to continue the hard work and have hope. And I was grateful that God was there to help me in my powerlessness to help her.

A Day-to-Day Life with Jesus

As I have written some of the stories of God's intervention in my life, I look back and am grateful and amazed at some of what I have seen Him do. But there are *way* more individuals who have experiences that are exceedingly more incredible than anything that has ever happened to me. It always surprises me as I talk to people who say "Why don't we see miracles today like in the Bible? If those are true, wouldn't we see them today?" Well, we do. They literally happen all the time. Friends and missionaries have exposed me to countless things they have experienced and witnessed . . . Many are readily available in testimonials on YouTube, in web searches, in books, and more. They are not hard to find. Hundreds of people being fed from a one pot of food, like when Jesus fed the five thousand from a few fishes and loaves. People being raised from the dead. Healings of various diseases and maladies. Exorcisms where people are delivered from evil spirits. Vision and hearing restored. Physical creative miracles, such as new eyes being created. Jesus appearing to Muslims and showing them that He is the true God. And more. It is still happening today.

By now you know my story is much more "normal" than those extreme examples. Many of the things I have shared, a lot of Christians have experienced. I also know many people whose journey with God has been mostly *without* the supernatural aspects in any kind of dramatic way. Their supernatural experience has more to do with the process of God being with them and changing their lives, and changing them from the inside out into more loving and healthier people. Almost seems like a natural, not supernatural, process.

But most of those who have not seen many miracles, if they have been closely walking with Him, will tell you that He is still very present and active in other ways, and especially one:

the connection and relationship they have with Him. Having Him always with them, and His being a source of strength and relationship. Seeing events in their lives being led along a path, doors opening as a result of prayer and provision, and a road that takes them on a trip that they know could only have been designed by Him.

I can tell you many, many times when I have prayed for healing and the person—including myself—was not healed. God works in His own ways, and His own time.

If you are someone who knows God, but have not had any or many of those experiences, don't feel like He is any less there or like you are somehow not as spiritual in some sort of way that diminishes your own faith journey or the presence of God in your life. He works in different ways with all of us.

God also promises something else if you do not know Him yet. He asks you to reach out and seek Him, and He says if you do that, you will find Him. One of my favorite verses says, "You will seek me and find me when you seek me with all your heart" (Jeremiah 29:13). He will reveal Himself to you in some way only God decides. Jesus said, "Seek and you will find" (Matthew 7:7). As I have shared, that is how it all happened with me, and that is true for many others I know, as well. When I reached out to Him, He did not suddenly appear. He had a friend call me. I interpreted that as Him—and it was true. The question is always, When He does show Himself to us in whatever way, will we see Him? Will we believe and respond?

So, when we hear stories and testimonies of how God has shown Himself to be real, it leads us to the biggest question of all, I believe. And one of the biggest questions of self-awareness. In my search for answers to all of my initial doubts, questions, and objections to faith, it was an anchoring realization that helped me find resolution to so many of my questions and doubts, and opened the door for a deeper connection with God. And that is what we will look at next.

Part III

How I Came to Believe through Science

Six

The Truth Is True

Our close friend for many years was at our house for a Sunday brunch, as we had asked several extended family members and friends to join us after I had spoken at church. Most were Christians, and some were not. This particular friend was one of my favorite people, and not a person of faith. But that had never gotten in the way of our friendship . . . we had been close for years.

We were standing in the kitchen when she said, "You know what I really like about your and your family's faith?" she asked.

"No . . . What is that?" I asked.

"I like the way it touches your whole life . . . the family, the ways you care about various charities . . . your values, how you raise your kids . . . and so on. It seems to just guide so much and I really like that. You can see how much good it does for you," she said. "But the thing I really like is that you never force it on others . . . like you don't push it on people. That's really nice. I like that a lot," she continued.

"Oh my gosh," I said . . . "I would never want to push it on anyone. Neither does God!" I chuckled. "He doesn't force Himself on anyone."

"Yeah," she said. "Like, it can be true for you, but not true for other people who have their own truth. You believe that it is true for you but not necessarily true for other people."

That caught my attention . . .

"Well, actually, I believe that it is not just true for *me*," I said. "I think it is *true*."

"You mean, like, *true*-true?'" she said, with a kind of shocked and puzzled expression.

"Yes," I said. "I do believe that is not just true for me, but it is *true*-true. Like *really* true."

She looked at me kind of like she couldn't believe I actually said that, and then she said, "But . . . there is no such thing as truth."

I looked at her for a moment . . . and said, "Including that statement?"

She just stared at me . . . pausing for a moment . . . and then said, "I never thought about it that way."

That moment was so profound. Her assertion that "there is no such thing as truth" just collapses upon itself. She says it like it is true . . . but if there is no such thing as objective truth, true reality, then she certainly can't make *that* statement, acting like that particular assertion can be true as it says nothing is true. And if that were the case, she can't even say "today is Sunday," or a lot of other things about objective reality. I am glad that the pilots on all our flights believe in objective truth, like up is up, down is down, and north is north. Ground is not air. And I am really glad they treat it as real. As "true-true."

Certainly there are ways that things are experienced by us, and we carry our perceptions, experiences, and interpretations as our "truth." That is our subjective reality. That's a very important concept in gaining different perspectives in many issues and events, and really important in psychotherapy and life, as people have often been gaslighted out of their own truth and experiences, and out of reality itself.

But there is also external, objective reality as well. I remember a grad student in statistics class angrily saying, "Well, I don't believe in the bell curve." Hmm. You might not like it, or you might have been adversely affected by how it was used sometime in a way you didn't think was fair, but, sorry . . . it is just an accounting of real numbers. It exists. You can tell me about your pain, but a statistical average is a statistical average.

In my friend's consideration of the "truth" of faith, she treats it as if it is a "personal truth" only . . . and has nothing to do with a real objective truth. But that could be a real problem if there really is a God who exists in objective reality and to whom it matters what we do with Him.

I said in the preface to this book that I am not just sharing my story so you can get to know me better, although that is important to me with my friends. The reason I have written this book is because I want you to know God. I don't want to try to "convert" in a weird or controlling way, as my friend in the preface said, but I want to invite you. That is what God does with us. He doesn't force us; he invites us into a relationship with Him. And as I have shared, when I accepted that invitation, my whole world changed.

But what must be understood is that this is more than just inviting us into a different "truth" for each of us. It is an invitation into not just another personal truth, but into what claims to be *the real objective truth about life and the universe.* When people examine the claims of Jesus, they find that He left absolutely zero room to interpret Him in any kind of "your truth/my truth" way. He left no room other than to decide whether or not He is absolutely who He said He is. We either believe Jesus is the Son of God as "true-true," or not. According to Him, it cannot be just "true for me," as my friend said. It is true for everyone, or not. That is what His message claims. As C. S. Lewis famously said: "A man who was merely a man and said the sort of things Jesus said would not be a great moral teacher. He would either be a lunatic—on the level with the man who says he is a poached egg—or else he would be the Devil of Hell. You must make your choice. Either this man was, and is, the Son of God, or else a madman or something worse."[1]

We are not talking about just another preference, or another philosophy of life that we might choose to adopt or not, with little consequence past whether or not "it works for me." What we are considering when we consider the claims of Christ is His claim to be ultimate, objective reality with the most significant benefits, and the most serious consequences. What is unique is His claim not just to be another choice on the buffet, true for one person and not for another, but a claim to be the ultimate objective truth. This faith's claim is to be the one true God. Period.

The examination of that truth can begin and proceed in a few different directions.

Personally, for me, I was not looking for objective evidence that Jesus was who He said He was in order to believe. That day when I walked into that church, I was not looking for the best intellectual argument for some religion or philosophy to live by. I was not investigating to find the "truth." I needed God to be "true-true." I needed Him to be objectively real and be able to help me. I was not looking for proof so I could believe. I was hoping it was objectively true, or "real," so I could find some help.

So, I really, really hoped and needed Him to actually exist and show up. I am glad He did, and thankfully, I have found Him to be real ever since.

But—and this is the other direction, after I had begun to follow Him and see His reality, as I described earlier in the book—I had some cognitive dissonance. I was now doing something that I had been taught in college and by others was "not true." My head was full of so-called facts I had been fed, such as "science disproves the Bible," "there are so many contradictions in the Bible," "there can't be such a thing as an all-powerful, good God if there are evil and suffering in the world," "Jesus can't be the real answer if so many of His followers are so mean and judgmental," "evolution disproves creation," "the church can't be true because it is always full of hypocrites," "all the church cares about is taking your money," and on and on. Now, was I finding myself believing in something that was stupid? Intellectually indefensible? It troubled me.

On the one hand, I could not negate the reality of what I was experiencing. God was showing Himself to be real. But what about all of this other stuff? Was I just supposed to stick my head in the sand?

I couldn't. So, I made a commitment. First, I would seek the reconciliation of this as best as I could, and second, I would only listen to people who actually knew something and were not just spouting opinions they had heard from someone else. As I reflected on a lot of what I had been told, I realized most of it was not from people who had actually examined the evidence or were from that particular field of expertise. It was from the circle of people I knew just in life, some professors who shared a lot of assumptions, but who later, when I went with information, were themselves totally unaware of the things they were putting down. They had kind of "bought the party line." They really didn't know what they were talking about. So, I went on a search.

The short summary of what was a long endeavor is that my questions were satisfied, over and over again. I found answers to the scientific quandaries, the philosophical questions, the historical questions, etc. I no longer have any cognitive dissonance about believing in Him and having to think I am denying science or whatever someone called their "objections." (I also surprisingly discovered research that showed that a substantial percentage of scientists believe in God and the number of scientists who believe in a personal God who answers prayer is the same as it was in 1900.) The believing scientists have no cognitive dissonance, either, and every day they live in those subjects, and most of them are a lot smarter than I am. Ask Francis Collins, the genius who unraveled the DNA code for several diseases, headed up the Human Genome Research Institute, and converted from atheism to Christianity. He himself decided as a scientist that he could not reject something without first studying it, getting the "data," so that is what he did. And when he actually studied the evidence, he became a Christian. For him, the evidence came first.

And, at the same time, even perfect evidence will never be enough to "make someone believe." There is another step, and that is to put one's faith into play. The intellect can only do so much . . . the heart and the spirit must get involved at some point. That is "faith." And nonbelievers are exercising faith just as much as believers. Science only observes what is there; faith takes the next step of answering how it got there. And scientists who are not believers take a step of faith as well in their explanations of how what they see was originated, as we shall see.

So, I came about this journey in reverse, if you will. Some look at the evidence for Jesus, and then decide to believe that He is real. I jumped in to see if He was there, and then I discovered the "evidence" answers after that. But, either way, both are important as to have a vibrant faith, our head and our heart work best when they are on the same team. We need the heart to take the step of faith, and we need the evidence, the Person of Jesus, to have faith "in." He was constantly offering evidence that He was who He said

He was, by miracles, by fulfilling prophecies that were thousands of years prior concerning the Messiah, by the life He lived and by his teachings themselves. I found that this was not a "blind leap of faith" that I had taken, but became an informed one that could stand up to the evidence.

But there is one more aspect to the role of understanding all of that scientific evidence that I discovered as mentioned above. When we study or try to crack the code on something finite and material, the natural world of science, such as cell biology, we pursue those endeavors to one day "figure it out." We can find out how a cell works. But examining the evidence of what exists, what science does, can never tell us where it came from, or "who" did it. It can only support it or point to it in various ways.

Plus, even if we decide or are convinced that a Creator must have made our world, in all its complexity—and to me there is no other reasonable explanation—once we try to fully understand God, we run into an unavoidable reality: we still will never totally understand Him. While there are many issues He does explain to us, there are so many other questions and things that He does and allows about which we ask "why?" or "how?" And what He says about that is very unsatisfactory to us at times:

> ***For my thoughts are not your thoughts, neither are your ways my ways . . . As the heavens are higher than the earth, so are my ways higher than your ways and my thoughts than your thoughts.*** (Isaiah 55: 8–9)

I had struggled with this reality, but then I came to the realization that it could be no other way. If I could totally understand Him, He would not be God. That would be like going to a university where you knew as much as every teacher. You'd do better to find a different school! Or find a different god.

In any case, it was a bit of a journey to settle down some of my mind's dilemmas, even after I was a believer. I found answers that put my doubts to rest, and I was free then to be comfortable with trusting a God whom I will never fully understand. So, let's hop into some of those areas where I had questions, some of the science and other obstacles for me, and then I will also share more about the one area of science where I can claim earned expertise and how it validated the Bible to me as well. So, I'd like to share with you some details about my own journey and how many of my questions were resolved for me.

Seven

Dynamic Tension and the Mind of Faith

In today's world, some parents feel that they are never going to "lie" to their kids and have them believe in Santa Claus or the Tooth Fairy. Well, I respect that. I understand that. I am just glad my parents didn't do that. ☺ I loved not being able to sleep past five on Christmas morning because my whole body was so alive waiting on my sister running in and saying, "Okay, it's time!" and I could finally race into the living room to see what Santa had brought. And the Tooth Fairy was a pretty good reward for having my tooth yanked out the night before. Thanks, guys! And I have to say, I never had my faith in God wrecked because I had been "lied" to as a child about Santa. I know some people feel differently; that's okay and I get it.

But, fairy tales have their place, I think. We need to hold on to the belief in the "ideal" world . . . like when a child goes to Disneyland, the "Magic Kingdom," for the first time. The hope for the ideal, since Plato and before, I think is an important human structure that drives us to wanting and achieving a better life. I hope I never lose that. We know from scientific research that optimists who see the world and the future in a positive light do better and achieve more than those who have a pessimistic view. That is a fact. Even in marriage, couples who see their spouses in a more positive light have better marriages. In a sense, they retain some of the honeymoon vision and appropriately delude themselves just a bit: "He is so scattered! Isn't that cute?" versus "What is wrong with you, you idiot? You never remember anything!" Just stay away from extreme denial, and don't overlook or enable bad behavior, but at the same time, keep it positive. That's a proven by research strategy in marriage, parenting, and business. Positivity wins. It is how we get to a better self and life. Thomas Edison kept trying (ten thousand times), believing the lights would eventually go on.

But what we are getting at here is a deep psychological structural reality: *mindset*. How we come to a subject, a person, or life itself has a lot to do with how we view it and, past that, how well we function. A positive mindset is important, but a childish view of the world is not. At some point, the highest-functioning people are able to deal with what psychologists call dynamic tension. That is the ability to hold polar opposites in tension in your mind and stay away from an "all good" or "all bad" view of self, others, and the world. Mature minds and personalities are able to integrate the good and the bad into one whole that has both.

The Bible says in the great love chapter, 1 Corinthians 13,

> ***When I was a child, I talked like a child, I thought like a child, I reasoned like a child. When I became a man, I put the ways of childhood behind me. For now we see only a***

> ***reflection as in a mirror; then we shall see face to face. Now I know in part; then I shall know fully, even as I am fully known.*** (vv. 11–12)

Profound. Children tend to have an idealistic view of the world, all things being equal. But as the verse says, we see only as a reflection in a mirror; our own views dictate most of how we look at things, a reflection of our own mindsets. Past that, though, the previous part of the verse is the meat here: at some point, we have to move from the cognitive mindset of a child to one of an adult. Adults who are mature see both the good and the bad, and can negotiate the whole of life without wanting an all-good life or person, to dealing with reality that has good aspects and sometimes some very bad realities. All-or-nothing thinking, as any psychologist will tell you, not only is immature thinking, but it also keeps us from seeing a lot of reality.

So, on to obstacles to faith. I begin this section with laying this groundwork of thinking because so many obstacles to faith come from our own mindsets versus the mindset of the Bible. I learned this in my own journey through my dilemmas of faith. I realized I must take the faith as it says it is, and then accept it or reject it accordingly. Like Francis Collins, the DNA scientist, said, I did not want to reject something this important without first examining it.

Earlier, I said that God has a marketing problem. If you watch adds on TV or Instagram, they will promise you a wonderful world: for a few dollars, you will get a perfect body. Or other marketing that just tells us all of the good stuff. "Buy our product, and you will be 'all good' or 'all well,' or 'all skinny' for all of time."

Not this God. He tells us the truth about the world, ourselves, others, and Himself. And, lousy marketing as it may seem to us, it is not all "happy talk." It is the real world as we really see it:

both good and bad exist together. No Disneyland fantasy reality. It is *real* reality. In fact, that was one of the things that made me believe even more easily. It hit me that I was looking with my own mindsets of wanting God and the world of the faith to be the way I wanted them to be, in my own childlike way of thinking, versus the way they really are. I wanted it to be all good, or one or the other. My mindset about God was omitting dynamic tensions in cognitive realties. And, as a psychologist, I know dynamic tensions are true! But in faith, I didn't want them to be.

Now, if that feels like a scolding of myself or perhaps you, hold on a minute. We all want the world to be perfect, other people to be perfect, and God to be the God that we wish He were. And the Bible says that is not your fault. And not only immature thinking at all . . . He is the one who set us up for that problem, in a certain way! The reason we think that way is that we are right . . . it all *should* be that, and even better than we can imagine. He really did create a better life than the one we have, with all of its problems. We had it in a perfect Creation, lost it when we left God, but He says it is coming back. And we all, believer or not, long for that lost Eden."

> ***I consider that our present sufferings are not comparable to the glory that will be revealed in us. The creation waits in eager expectation for the revelation of the sons of God. For the creation was subjected to futility, not by its own will, but because of the One who subjected it, in hope that the creation itself will be set free from its bondage to decay and brought into the glorious freedom of the children of God. We know that the whole creation has been groaning together in the pains of childbirth until the present time. Not only that,***

> ***but we ourselves, who have the firstfruits of the Spirit, groan inwardly as we wait eagerly for our adoption as sons, the redemption of our bodies. For in this hope we were saved; but hope that is seen is no hope at all. Who hopes for what he can already see? But if we hope for what we do not yet see, we wait for it patiently.*** (Romans 8:18–29 BSB)

As Solomon said, "He has also set eternity in the human heart; yet no one can fathom what God has done from beginning to end" (Ecclesiastes 3:11).

Crap . . . we are in a cognitive dilemma. He made us to think of and long for and groan for a perfect life all the time, a life that does not have pain, poverty, loss, cruelty, bad people, or the like. Just like a hungry person longs for food even when he does not have it, we long for a better world. And worse than that, as Solomon said, we cannot understand what He is doing in the big picture, from beginning to end!

So, what is it that we can understand that helped me resolve many of the obstacles that we are going to look at? Simply put,

We are not living in the world as it was meant to be.

We can envision a better world and life than the one we find ourselves in. We can envision the "ideal." Yet, we are very clearly aware of the badness and evil that exist. But many times, our rejection of faith is because we are looking at faith in a way where we intellectually lose the dynamic tension of the reality of the way this world is, that there is beauty and goodness, while at the same time, the existence of much evil and pain. We want it to be an ideal or "all-good" world and reject the faith with objections like "if God is good and loving, then how can suffering exist?" But the Bible does not lose that tension. It says the world was created to be ideal, and then when we rejected God, the goodness was infected with evil as a result. Now, from the Bible's explanation, we have both. And that fits reality. If we are rejecting God because badness exists, we are not rejecting the story of the Bible. We are demanding a world that not only does not exist, but that the Bible does not claim exists, either. It says that both are true and explains what we see. But sometimes, in examining faith, we demand it to be one or the other. A God who only allows good. A world where there is only good and no suffering, and if there is suffering, there cannot be a God. Or people who claim to follow Jesus would all be like Him if He were truly "the Way" and if He were truly "real."

But when we reject the God of the Bible and Jesus as God for those reasons, we are rejecting something that we have made up. That is not the God of the Bible. Remember? He has a "marketing problem" in that He does not lie to us, like advertisers do, and say that it is going to be all good. At least not yet. But—and this is the important part—He tells us the real story of *why* we have both, the wish for the ideal, and yet the reality of good gone bad.

He tells us we long for perfection because we were designed for exactly that. We are not designed to be able to tolerate or understand the knowledge (awareness and experience) of good and evil. "Don't eat of *that* tree," we were told. We were designed for the ideal. And now we are in both, exactly what He told us not to do. When a parent says, "Don't touch the hot stove, or you will know what a burn feels like," she is not kidding. And then, if we do touch it, we know. That is the reality where we live now.

So if we examine the faith as the faith presents itself, it holds true to its message. And we can either accept that or reject it. It says that your longing for perfection and the absence of evil and suffering are real and valid and there for a reason. *And* your experience of the opposite is real and valid, and your hatred for evil is valid also. *And* it gives the best explanation for what we find to be reality than any other philosophy or religion by far. But it does not give us the option of rejecting it, because it promises something that we just made up, that this life now should be all good, in order to have been created by a loving God.

But here is the good news. (Interesting tidbit: "gospel" actually means "good news.") The good news is that the Bible not only provides a reality picture of the faith as believing that good and bad both exist here, but it also tells us that your longing does have an answer, and it will be forthcoming. And what many Christians experience, and my story is included, is that when we enter into that faith, we progressively find the answer to that longing being experienced along the way in increasing measure, until one day it will all be made right in the totality. There is a heaven. There is a Second Coming, where all justice will be served and all things made right that we long to be right. And now, it is possible to begin to experience more of that future reality through a relationship with Him.

So, as we enter into some of these objections and the answers that satisfied me which I will share from the Bible, I invite you to look at them from a higher cognitive place of being able to hold a dynamic tension in your head, to hold polar opposites in your head as both being able to be true. Up and down, right and left, and good and bad. If you do that, then you will be able to at least examine the answers from a place where they totally can make sense and there can be a good God, along with the existence of evil. That is what helped me, when I had to look at the real world as it exists, and the faith as it presents itself, and see if the evidence of this life matched the evidence I see in real life.

Eight

Science as an Obstacle to Faith

After taking the "faith step" I took in my college awakening, I did have some nagging questions in my brain about what I had done, even as I was experiencing God as real. There were so many smart people who said that being a Christian is "intellectual suicide." As I heard someone say one time, "If a Christian had a brain cell, it would die of loneliness."[1] I was in college, and my professors were telling us that all of that church stuff some of us grew up with is a bunch of myths. Was I an idiot for believing it? I had to settle that in my head . . . what I was experiencing as true versus people telling me it wasn't. Spiritual gaslighting, if you will. They said that science had disproved the Bible, and yet I was experiencing it as real.

What I found as I began digging in were two things. First, when I got into the science, there were answers by scientists and other areas of academic inquiry themselves. There were tons of scientists, historians, philosophers, business experts, and the like who look at the evidence and say that it supports the faith. I learned that faith was not a matter of "IQ" at all. Many geniuses believe it. Second, a lot of what was intellectually "non-defensible" was a faith that is *not* what the Bible actually says, but misconceptions that people have been told or, unfortunately, what they had seen or experienced with Christians. I found that what people were rejecting was not even the real faith. It had more to do with organized religion or common wrongs that are shouted from pulpits and taught in churches every day. In fact, I discovered that much of the time, *the Bible agreed with the critics.* It was really encouraging to find out that to be a follower of Jesus, I did not have to believe things I knew were goofy. At this point in my life, I have written several psychology and personal growth books for Christians to show how many of the teachings of "Christians" are damaging to mental health and certainly not the teachings of the Bible.

This book is not intended to be an exhaustive work on the intellection basis for Christian belief; it is rather a sharing of my *own* personal journey, including the intellectual barriers to faith that I personally experienced. My hope is that through sharing this journey, including the specific intellection conflicts I experienced, you too can discover that objections are resolvable.

THE SCIENCE OF ORIGINS . . . WHERE DID IT ALL COME FROM?

The Bible says that there was a beginning to Creation in Genesis. God spoke all of this into being out of nothing. As they say in the Latin, "ex nihilo." The material universe, according to the Bible, came from an *immaterial* source, a Person, God. In the Bible's presentation, there was something that was "eternal" and that was God, *not* this physical universe.

Most atheism says that the universe was what was always there. It is eternal, unless you go with the really, really big step of faith and believe that there was nothing, and nothing all of a sudden produced the material that the universe came from. No eternal God, nor eternal material, but *nothing*. Somehow, once, something came from nothing. Most don't hold to that . . . it takes a really, *really* large blind leap of faith.

So, the big two options that disagree are eternal God versus eternal material. Some "uncaused cause." Then, the two sides begin to agree. They both believe there was indeed a beginning. It is called the "Big Bang," which is where and when the universe began. This is very important because it shows us how old it is, 13.77 billion years is the most believed age, and that shows us that it is a finite universe that is expanding. That kind of logically kills the idea that the universe itself was eternal since astronomers and physicists can show that it did have a beginning. *If something had a beginning, then something caused it.* Everything with a beginning has a cause. The universe we live in had an actual cause, a beginning. So, the universe was not always there. It *began* to be there.

That does not mean, though, that everything has to have a cause, like an eternal God.

But only things that had a beginning, like this material universe that has a known beginning. So, what caused it? It had to be something outside of it, and that is exactly what the Bible says.

After reading all of the different positions, I came to believe exactly what many of the astrophysicists and astronomers say: "*Someone* had to have done this." The ones who don't say that are usually still holding fast to the their *assumption* and hard held belief that "since there is no God, it must have happened in a way we just don't understand." Realize this: that is not science, but a faith position also, just like believing that it was God who did it. If someone has already determined there is no God, they will look at the evidence and go that direction. If someone is open to His existence, the evidence can certainly more than support that view. It leads one to it.

NOT RANDOM, BUT PRECISELY ORDERED BY SOMEONE TO EXIST

The next thing I learned about all of this "where did it all come from" was the reality of the incredible "fine-tuning" of the universe that makes it possible to exist as it is, as well as makes it possible for it to have life. It is amazingly and delicately balanced among multiple factors. As Dr. Dennis Scania, head of Cambridge University Observatories, said, "If you change a little bit the laws of nature, or you change a little bit the constants of nature—like the charge on the electron—then the way the universe develops is so changed, it is very likely that intelligent life would not have been able to develop."[2] Dr. Paul Davies, professor of theoretical physics at Adelaide University, put it: "The really amazing thing is not that life on Earth is balanced on a knife edge, but that the entire universe is balanced on a knife edge, and would be total chaos if any of the natural 'constants' were off even slightly. You see, even if you dismiss man as a chance happening, the fact remains that the universe seems unreasonably suited to the existence of life—almost contrived—you might say a 'put-up job.'"[3]

Or Sir Fred Hoyle, an English astronomer who formulated the theory of stellar nucleosynthesis, said these things about fine-tuning: "A commonsense interpretation of the facts suggests that a superintendent has monkeyed with the physics, as well as chemistry and biology, and that there are no blind forces worth speaking about in nature. I do not believe that any physicist who examined the evidence could fail to draw the inference that the laws of nuclear physics have been deliberately designed with regard to the consequences they produce within stars."[4]

A remembrance of Hoyle by John Horgan published in *Scientific American* said, "Hoyle also suspected that life and indeed the entire universe must be unfolding according to some cosmic plan. The universe is an 'obvious fix,' Hoyle said. 'There are too many things that look accidental which are not.' When I asked if Hoyle thought some supernatural intelligence is guiding things, he nodded gravely. 'That's the way I look on God. It is a fix, but how it's being fixed I don't know.'"[5]

A. L. Van Den Herik writes about the problem of how to explain the fine-tuning of the many physical constants that make up the laws of physics and the universe if it just appeared without a Creator. She says, "Astrophysicist Hugh Ross has listed dozens of characteristics of the universe that must be set with extreme precision, such that a minuscule change in any of them would disrupt the balance of the universe enough to prevent it from existing at all. For example, Ross states: 'Unless the number of electrons is equivalent to the number of protons to an accuracy of one part in 10^{37} [one followed by thirty-seven zeros] or better, electromagnetic forces in the universe would have so overcome gravitational forces that galaxies, stars, and planets never would have formed.'"[6]

The quotes could go on and on, but you get the idea. The universe and existence of life in the universe are so precise, to unbelievable odds if happening by chance, that many scientists over and over have concluded that there is no possible way that it "just happened" without a designer.

Herik cites Ross's description of these odds:

> *Suppose we cover an area of land equivalent to one million North American continents with dimes up to the height of the moon (239,000 miles). We then mix in one dime that has been painted red and ask a blindfolded friend to pick out one dime. The chance that your friend would select the red dime is one in 10^{37}, the same probability that the "just right" ratio of protons*

> *to electrons in atoms happened by chance alone (that is, without any guidance by "someone turning the knobs" to make it that way).*[7]

I can't do that math, but it seems like an extreme chance to me. And the parameters he is describing there in terms of electrons' equivalency to protons requiring accuracy to that degree is only one of many precise parameters that are required to be "just right" for all of this to exist. I began to think the chances of that happening without a designer in a random explosion takes more faith than I have. The design argument is simple, yet the specific evidence was so deep and complex that the argument proved irrefutable to me: when you see design, there has to have been a designer, especially design this complex and precise to subatomic levels.

Even if you had all of the raw material of a Rolex watch in a paper bag unassembled (which is a big assumption even for that to happen by chance . . . having just the right pieces made of just the right metal of just the right shapes, sizes, and weights, all together in a paper bag) and threw them up in the air, the chances of them landing perfectly assembled in working order are not even imaginable. Much less to give you the accurate time that day! And if you find a Rolex watch on the beach, you would not ever think that it formed itself by chance. You naturally would know there was a designer who put all of that together to work the way it works. You would wonder who dropped it there, too. Although these are astrophysicists who are figuring out all of these complicated components and elements and how they fit together, it is not rocket science to figure out that the design speaks to a Designer. And that is exactly what the "rocket scientists" themselves say: it had to have a designer.

We could go on and on about the design of the universe and the incredible scientific evidence that points to a designer. But it made sense to me as it pointed to what the Bible says about this issue:

> ***They know the truth about God because he has made it obvious to them. For ever since the world was created, people have seen the earth and sky. Through everything God made, they can clearly see his invisible qualities—his eternal power and divine nature. So they have no excuse for not knowing God. Yes, they knew God, but they wouldn't worship him as God or even give him thanks. And they began to think up foolish ideas of what God was like.*** (Romans 1:19–21 NLT)

When you compare that passage from the New Testament to this quote from Arno Penzias, Nobel Laureate in physics and codiscoverer of the radiation afterglow from the Big Bang, it appears that over and over, science and the Bible agree:

> *Astronomy leads us to a unique event, a universe which was created out of nothing, one with the very delicate balance needed to provide exactly the conditions required to permit life, and which has an underlying (one might say "supernatural") plan.*[8]

The scientists and the Bible say the same thing.

DOWN TO EARTH

We could look at much more evidence from the skies above that I enjoyed discovering, as far as outer space goes, but for sake of our "space" limitations (no pun intended), let's look at some of the design revealed in other areas of science that got my attention back in my early days of faith. Instead of breaking down all of the subspecialties to a great degree, I want to talk briefly about a huge problem that exists if you try to explain the earth and life without God.

That problem is the dependence that all of creation has on systems and interrelatedness, and how those systems could exist without a Designer above them. This has nothing to do with the evolution versus non-evolution debate that some have. (I personally don't care if you think God did it in an instant or if he designed it as a slowly evolving plan. Both of those positions require Him, and belief in Him is what is important to me.) Let's just assume, since many people do, that everything started with primordial goo and then evolved into greater and greater complexity and even complex systems. The question has to do with whether or not those complex systems we see and live by could have become like they are on their own, without an external designer and organizer of those systems. The evolutionary scientists of faith say that "God did it" is the only possible rational explanation, and the materialists say "evolution must have done it alone since there is no God." They just don't know how. Both of those conclusions require faith. A belief.

The design scientists argue that this increasing high-order complexity is impossible without a designer. And non-design scientists say that all of this must have happened by random mutations without design. Mutations getting lucky in that they fit another mutation way across the meadow. That is the argument they have back and forth. One will talk about a complex system where parts are dependent on other parts and say the parts could not have developed in just the needed way and come together to form something more complex without each other communicating. To develop, the system parts have to have the needs of each other "in mind" as they were developing themselves. They say the work of a designer shaping them to fit one another is necessary, since the parts have no relationship, yet others will show tiny examples of mutations that actually do occur without design, and then they say that they randomly were able to continue to develop into more and more complex systems by themselves through natural selection. The one that works best wins. The "part" had a lucky mutation randomly, and it randomly built something more complex to fit with another random part. A steering wheel mutated into a steering wheel without having relationship to a chassis of a car . . . yet somehow it evolved into a perfect fit for the car without a designer knowing what each part would need from the other.

I am a layman, but I just promised to tell you the answers that satisfied me. I felt like, as I studied it, the chances of all of those complex systems happening to work together through one piece getting lucky and mutating in a way that would fit with another part that also got lucky, and then that changing the software code (DNA) to be installed in the operating system to eventually turn a monkey into Einstein with no designer, is too big a stretch for me. Especially when you realize that the code had to be written for the organism to later reproduce itself . . . but, it had to exist before it wrote the code to reproduce itself, so how did it get produced to think ahead and write a code to reproduce? There are many such problems for me with a non-designer viewpoint.

When I was looking at this design problem in the creation, I would think of systems way simpler than a human, or even a human cell. Again, take for example, a car. And while I know there are atheistic answers offered to this quandary, for me, having a designer makes much more sense. (I think they have more faith than I do.) The engine needs parts that are designed for one another, just like the human body does. The fuel tank has to be there, and the fuel lines, ready to work. A fuel pump that gets the gas to the cylinder is required, and it has to be precisely designed to do that job with the gas and the cylinder it is going to work with, but it had to be designed precisely right, having no relationship with them at the time. Just by chance, designed itself perfectly to work with those other parts? (We can't even hope for a Toyota part to work with a Ford.) The carburetor has to mix the gas and air perfectly so it is just right for burning, not too lean or rich, and that mixture is pulled into the cylinder just right, where it is ignited with a spark at just the right timing. (Not to mention the proper octane gas to exist separate from this whole process, back to the order of the universe.) The combustion creates the energy that drives the driveshaft, which is connected to the wheels, which allow movement, which are in turn are guided by another system (the steering system) to get you moving in the right direction (if some designer put a road down for you). And if you have to stop, then there is the braking system in the car as well, although the brakes did not know the engine that would maybe move the car too fast one day and they might be needed, but they evolved themselves into those perfect parts randomly on their own, hoping to one day find a job?

I find this explanation extraordinarily difficult to believe.

Your brain alone has nearly 100 billion neurons that work together, and the human body has trillions of cells. Tens of trillions. The brain has tens of billions of neurons that carry the messages with the information needed for your body to do what it needs to do. They provide the information for pain, touch, position, etc. Working together. Sensory neurons get the info, like "you just touched something hot." Motor neurons then give commands to muscles and various organs and glands to do something, like move your hand away from the fire. Dendrites receive information, and axons send and convey it. They do this in an "in-between space" called the synapse through neurotransmitters, chemical messengers, that are somehow able to carry those messages in an electrical soup mixture with just the right levels of soup in the "bowl," the synapse. And those chemicals have to be just the right chemicals to be able to make that work . . . they can't be a chocolate milkshake or any other mixture. Dopamine is dopamine, and serotonin is serotonin. Good thing it just happened to be there in that synapse when needed. Oh . . . and good thing the food just happens to exist on the earth for your body to make it just correctly.

We could go on to greater complexities, which there are, especially when you get to cell construction and functioning. But to me, all of this developing without a designer and these systems working together just is way past what I have the faith to believe. Then all of this wiring has to function perfectly along with the organs and muscles and glands. This extremely complicated wiring system itself has to be right, taking highly trained neurologists to even understand it, much less work on it. I just could not believe that all of this just happened, or evolved, without a designer. Can you open up the motherboard to a computer (which is much, much less complicated) and think it could just happen? Great painting, but there has to be a Picasso (artist) somewhere. Great ceiling, Sistine Chapel . . . but without a Michelangelo painting it? I just could not believe that was possible.

I kept thinking about it. Eyes . . . they let light in and do a lot of complicated stuff with it. Light comes in through the cornea and hits the lens, and then (amazingly) your pupil gets larger or smaller in order to control the amount of light it lets in (think of a doorman at a bar). And there just happens to be a cornea and lens that bend the light to make it come into focus. Light hits the retina in the rear, and the retina changes the images into electrical signals and then back to the nerves; the optic nerve takes them to the brain to a specific area that takes care of vision. By the way, the optic nerve carries all of those signals from both eyes at once and the brain integrates all of that together into one image. Oh yeah . . . make sure the eye is properly lubricated and has some window shades and windshield wipers that automatically without your conscious attention blink every certain amount of seconds, as needed. Even Darwin said, "The eye to this day gives me a cold shudder."[9] He realized that chance mutations would be a tough road to get to an eye.

Need energy to run this machine, this body? No problem . . . just make sure you have a tongue that has taste buds of various kinds that happen to match the "tastes" that are available in the outside world in food that is your fuel. That way you will know it is right to take into the machine. And because you like it, you are going to be motivated to take the food in because just the anticipation of it has already sent messages of glandular stimulation to your mouth to produce saliva to begin to process it. (How is that for an advance delivery system? "Incoming missile.") If it passes the taste test, you just so happen to have teeth shaped correctly that can process the delivery and get it ready and able to be swallowed.

Swallowing is no big deal since your brain has sent messengers to your throat to take care of that job and it moves muscles to propel it downward through the esophagus, skipping your windpipe, hopefully, because the tunnel system "luckily" has the proper lanes and your epiglottis manages the traffic, into your stomach which "someone" alerted to have juices waiting to begin breaking all of that firewood into burnable bits for fuel. And it will get there fine, because your upper stomach got the memo to relax and let the food enter, and the lower stomach will mix it all up with those digestive juices. (By the way, it needed some help from your pancreas and liver for those juices to be right . . . another system that volunteered its talents to make it all go well.)

But you won't need all that firewood . . . just the nutrients. No worries, your system knows what to keep and what to throw away, called "waste." And you happen to have a function in your small intestine that will absorb the water from all of the food being processed and put the nutrients into your bloodstream (an entirely different vascular system) that will deliver them where they are needed throughout the body, and then turn all of that liquid left-over mess into something solid called a stool. That is then sent to your rectum, where it is stored for a while until you have a moment to find a magazine, sit down, and get rid of it.

Plus, all of this needed quite a bit of help from some other systems, nerves, and hormones to control this entire process. One system of systems of lots of separate parts, which, by the way, work perfectly together, interacting with entire other systems to make just one process required for life, fueling, work. Regularly, every single day, on a kind of rhythm (hopefully).

I hope you forgive my tongue-in-cheek bit sarcastic tone here, but seriously. When I started to look at only an evolutionary process doing all of this *without* a designer, I just had to cut bait. And, fortunately, I found many scientists who knew way more than me agreeing, on *scientific* grounds, not just common sense. (I am amazed when I hear people say "I don't believe in God; I believe in 'Science,'" when so so many of the scientists they are believing in believe in God!)

Want to have another little model of you? How about that reproductive system? Penises and vaginas that are already perfectly equipped to do what they do without people needing much training at all, wired at the factory, to start the process (even way before it might be wise). And that begins with a somewhat spiritual, nonphysical dynamic called "connection" through "attraction," which we will examine in the psychology section. But beginning with just sight, seeing a body, then seeing a pair of eyes, conversation, pupils dilating to bodies embracing and taking it from there, the reproductive system has a lot of moving parts, as I mentioned in a previous chapter. The point again is this: all of these parts magically fit and work together very well. Just as if they were made for each other. Separate items that fit each other perfectly to do for each other what the other needs to be done in order to make its function work! Get the sperm truck to show up at the factory and get the factory's permission. Deliver the sperm, take it in to where an egg has just so happened to be visiting for a few days that time of month, and go on from there. Glad to know there is a brain somewhere already saving up for school clothes. Takes a village of "systems" to make life work. And how did one part get to be the perfect part the other would need with no relationship between them at all as each was "randomly" evolving without a designer along the way?

It was the cognitive dissonance of my having heard that "evolution and science had done away with the need for God" that got me studying all of this in the beginning. And the more I learned about complexity in the sciences, the more I knew that whether God did it in a moment or through eons of time (and even Christians and Christian scientists have different views on that), it was undeniable there was a very complex design to all of these systems working together. Even Darwin said the eye made him shudder. Nowhere do we see that kind of design happening at anything approaching that level without an architect behind it.

Very smart scientists, for complicated brainiac scientific reasons, said the same thing.

I had to admit something for myself. Even if I did not *want* to believe, which I did, I don't think I could help it. I would have to believe, and the "fear of God" would be in me just from the science. After looking at the science, I just cannot *not* believe. I find myself with Einstein, who said, "I believe in Spinoza's God, Who reveals Himself in the lawful harmony of the world."[10]

Nine

Can I Trust the Bible?

Back in college, when I was grappling with these issues of my faith, I had changed my major to psychology and was headed in a totally new direction in life and also in academia. This put me in the science building a lot, and also around brilliant professors and students. The science world had a very different feel from the business school, where I had been my first two years. But one of the really different feelings was how I felt being identified now as a Christian and frequently having a Bible with my stack of books in that setting. I knew everyone was looking at me like I was a superstitious idiot. I have to admit to feeling a bit squeamish.

I could walk in there today and not feel squeamish at all for one simple reason: I feel very secure about this book, the Bible, being true. But that change didn't happen overnight. It was a process of lots of study and learning how dependable the Bible actually is and, over time, how much it continues to be proven trustworthy.

Given the space here, I can't write a full defense of the dependability of the Bible in history, prophecy, archaeology, and other disciplines. But, again, what I want to do is just share with you the things I learned in my early days of faith that taught me to trust it as God's Word to us. And in a later chapter, I will go deeper into how much I even trusted it more as the years went on because of the field of psychology and the ways that it proved the truth of the Bible to me. So, let's look at what helped me first.

CAN WE TRUST THE BIBLE AS GOD'S INSPIRED WORD?

My beginning question, and it was a big one, was whether I could trust the Scriptures as truth. The Scriptures claim to be God's Word, His communication about Himself to us, about life, and about salvation. So many people had strong opinions that said the opposite: "full of myths, inaccuracies, contradictions," etc. So how did I come to believe that I could believe it? Especially the New Testament? Here are just a few facts that settled my doubts.

Historical Accuracy of the Bible

In terms of having faith in Jesus as Lord and Savior, which is the biggest issue of the Bible, we have to believe the biblical record about Him. How do we know the New Testament record is true?

One way is by knowing when it was written. Critics used to say that so much time had passed between when He actually lived and the New Testament was written that the story morphed and contains a lot of myths in it. Actually, archaeology has proven that wrong. William F. Albright, who was the world's foremost biblical archaeologist, said this: "In my opinion, every book of the New Testament was written by a baptized Jew between the forties and the eighties of the first century A.D. (very probably sometime between about 50 and 75 A.D.)."[1] Apologist Josh McDowell writes, "Sir William Ramsay, one of the greatest archaeologists ever to have lived . . . conceded that Acts could not be a second-century document but was rather a mid-first-century account."[2] He also writes, "Dr. John A. T. Robinson's conclusions in his new book *Redating the New Testament* are startlingly radical. His research led to the conviction that the whole of the New Testament was written before the Fall of Jerusalem in A.D. 70."[3]

These facts are a big deal because the records of the life of Jesus and the facts surrounding His miracles and resurrection and teachings were written and widely distributed while actual eyewitnesses were still alive and around. Imagine major newspapers and television networks reporting that Taylor Swift had claimed to be God and the Messiah, and rose from the dead after performing many miracles and being crucified by the record industry in Times Square while people who lived in NYC are still around. All of those people in NYC who knew that to not be true would kill that story, and for sure, you would read many, many other articles talking about how false it was.

Plus, many of His followers were beginning a movement, and they were being persecuted and dying because they believed it is true. That would have been easily refuted, and no one would even do it to begin with. Go out and die for believing that Taylor Swift was the messiah? Or Tom Brady? Or anyone else who didn't actually prove it? Dying for it when you knew you hadn't seen it happen? Many of the early eyewitnesses to Jesus being alive after his resurrection went on to be tortured and killed for holding on to their account of what they had seen.

As Albright writes, "Only modern scholars who lack both historical method and perspective can spin such a web of speculation as that with which form-critics have surrounded the Gospel tradition."[4] He also wrote, "All we can say is that period of between twenty and fifty years is too slight to permit of any appreciable corruption of the essential content and even of the specific wording of the sayings of Jesus."[5] As of this writing, that would be like making up stories about Sting or Michael Jordan that are mythical fabrications and selling them as things that really happened. People were there and know better.

Further, McDowell goes on to say, "Jeffery L. Sheler, religion writer for *US News & World Report*, writes, 'The Bible and its sources remain firmly grounded in history.'"[6] The gospels clearly pass the tests that we use to scrutinize any writings of antiquity. No one doubts Aristotle's writings, and the earliest copy we have of those were nearly 1,400 years after his death, and only forty-nine manuscripts exist. Caesar's history of the Gallic Wars was written between 58 and 50 BC, and we only have nine of ten copies dating a thousand years after his death. At this time, there are over 5,600 Greek manuscripts that have been found. In the newer edition of the book, Wallace cites one of the world's leading authorities on the Greek text and New Testament manuscripts, Daniel B. Wallace, who said, "Well over 200 biblical manuscripts (90 of which are New Testament) were discovered in the Sinai in 1975 when a hidden compartment of St. George's Tower was uncovered. Some of these manuscripts are quite ancient. They [the recent manuscript discoveries] all confirm that the transmission of the New Testament has been accomplished in relative purity and that God knows how to preserve the text from destruction. In addition to the manuscripts, there are 50,000 fragments sealed in boxes. About 30 separate New Testament manuscripts have been identified in the fragments, and scholars believe there may be many more."[7]

Sir Frederic Kenyon, former director and principal librarian at the British Museum, said to be the leading authority on ancient manuscripts, says, "The interval then between the dates of original composition and the earliest extant evidence becomes so small as to be in fact negligible, and the last foundation for any doubt that the

Scriptures have come down to us substantially as they were written has now been removed. Both the authenticity and the general integrity of the books of the New Testament may be regarded as finally established."[8]

I believe that the Bible is a trustworthy record of the life of Jesus and the story of God, and that if we can trust anything from the literature of antiquity, we can trust the Bible. In addition, there are many extrabiblical (nonbiblical) secular historians writing at the same time who talk about Jesus and the movement (see for example, Josephus, Tacitus, Pliny the Younger, Phlegon, Thallus, Suetonius, Lucian, etc.). People do not have to believe that only the Bible talks about Jesus, and that is how we know he was real. The historians of the time were writing about him as well.

Prophecy Fulfilled

One of the realities that gave me confidence in the Bible and specifically in Jesus' claim to be the Messiah was its ability to predict the future accurately. Written by around forty authors, over a period of 1,500 to 2,000 years, it is remarkable that it has sixty-six books that all carry the exact same spiritual narrative and message in different ways. The Bible is consistent throughout all of those books and authors. And more than that, the entire Bible points to one Person: Jesus the Messiah.

The Jews of the first century were among a long list of people waiting on the coming of the Messiah, which had been foretold for a long, long time. And then, this Person Jesus shows up and says, "I am He." How are we to know, and how were they to know that He was the long-awaited one?

We begin with the eyewitnesses and the lives of His followers who knew Him, and their history and the history of the early church as it was progressing alongside them, and the persecution of those followers by the political and religious systems of the first century. These were real people. We also have the record of His life, and the predictions of this coming Messiah, the Jewish Savior. The fact is this: He fulfilled all of the Old Testament prophecies of the coming Messiah.

That is why He said to those religious leaders who refused to believe Him, "If you believed Moses, you would believe Me, because He wrote of Me" (John 5:46 BSB). And Moses was by far not the only one who wrote of the Messiah who would come. Many other Old Testament authors did as well, very specifically, and the Jews were always waiting for their Messiah to come.

Jesus fulfilled somewhere around three hundred specific prophecies that were written long before He came about the coming King, by many authors who were separated in time. I won't list all of them here, but just to name a few of how detailed and specific they are:

- He would be born in Bethlehem.
- A messenger would come before him (John the Baptist).
- He would be betrayed by His own friend (Judas).
- He would be betrayed for thirty pieces of silver (Judas).
- His betrayal money would be spent in a specific way (to the potter's field).
- He would die by crucifixion.
- In death, his clothes would be divided by the casting of lots.
- He would have specific wounds in His crucifixion.
- He would be given vinegar on the cross.
- His hands and feet would be pierced.
- He would mingle with sinners and be buried with the rich (convicted criminals on the cross and the tomb given by Joseph of Arimathea).

- He would triumph over Satan and be bruised but would win (crucified but resurrected, and Satan defeated by his resurrection).
- He would be born by the seed of a woman (virgin birth from Mary and the Holy Spirit).
- He would come from specific lineage.
- He would triumphantly enter Jerusalem on a donkey (Palm Sunday).
- And many, many, many more.

It became clear to me that only a supernatural book inspired by God could make that many predictions that were fulfilled by one specific person. It was just one more building block that said to me this book was the real deal. And, as I researched the apparent contradictions in the Bible, it became clear to me that they are readily understandable, such as different eyewitness accounts that tell a different view of the same incident. What is important is that the incidents and events happened in all of the accounts.

Nowhere in the Bible is there a contradiction of the central message or important points. One gospel writer might report a different number of angels than the other at the tomb. If I saw you and a few other people at a concert, I might say to a mutual friend, "I saw Heather at the concert." A friend who was with me might tell someone, "I saw Heather and Sarah at the concert." No contradiction other than what one emphasizes versus another. But never do you see someone saying "He died and was placed in a tomb" and someone else saying "He didn't die after the cross, he went fishing." Those kinds of contradictions are not there, the kind that would make us question the main message it is trying to convey.

A similar criticism some people have is about all the different denominations and theologians getting very different things from the Bible and believing very different things. And "so many translations . . . you can't believe it." But we have the original language those translations come from. Translators translate the original Hebrew and Greek texts differently, but the originals are what they are, period.

And there are different denominations . . . that is true . . . in some ways and yet not in others. For all of the "denominations" who would fall into what is commonly called "orthodox," they all believe in the same essentials of the faith and agree on them. unless they are some strange cult. Then, just as the Bible predicts they will and did from the beginning of the church, some do differ on various interpretations or emphases on things and go their separate ways. (Which I think often is dumb to make a new denomination over such little issues, but each to their own.) But all of those denominations would still all agree on 90 percent of the rest of the "main" message. Different orthodox denominations emphasize different minor points.

Each to their own, and the Bible itself says people will disagree on some minor issues, what is called "disputable" issues (Romans 14:1), and allows for it, as long as they believe the essentials: Jesus is who He said He was, died, and was resurrected, and we are reconnected to God through believing in Him. That is the gospel.

MIRACLES

When I first came to deeper faith in college, I had always believed in the Bible, although in a very not-very-informed way. But something that had always been lurking in the background, which in my "faith-light" youth years had not bothered me that much, were the miracles that were supposed to have happened in the Bible. I was told by people as a child that those were true, but God didn't do that stuff anymore. Those were for "biblical times." Now we have doctors, for example, and God doesn't need to do those. And the miracles were for Jesus to prove who He said he was when He was on earth. That was fine with me, since I just wanted to play golf anyway. Digging into biblical dilemmas back then was not my thing. I could believe they happened then and not now without much distress.

But all of a sudden, I was getting serious about this stuff and basing my life on it all being true. So, what about all of these miracles?

But this didn't make sense to me. Why wouldn't He continue to do miracles today? The New Testament even *says* He would. So, "What gives?" I wondered.

I found out.

My first intro was when I read a few books I already mentioned, then many others, which told the stories of God doing miraculous things today. Then, I had a few of my own supernatural experiences early on. But, as I continued to investigate, I really found the answer to "Why don't we see the things we read about in the Bible occurring today?"

The answer is, "We do." They happen every day around the world.

They literally happen all the time, and, little did I know, they are easily findable. My first source way back then was reading books containing spiritual memoirs and personal journeys that gave accounts of all sorts of miracles, just like in the Bible. Then I began to go to churches to hear speakers tell their stories and testimonies.

I also began to hear about an abundance of miracles when I started to work with a lot of missionaries and missions organizations. I have met and know so many people who have told me of the miracles they have seen, some very regularly, of dramatic healings, creative miracles (such as eyes being created in a person blind from birth right in front of them), visions, actual people being raised from the dead (I just visited with a missionary whom I know well and is credible, whose wife was dead for two days in the morgue and was resurrected), appearances of angels and demons, and "feeding of the five thousand"–type miracles from a tiny bit of food as Jesus did. Incredible miracles do happen today, all over the world.

You will find some who have other interpretations of those events, like my friend to whom I told the kneecap healing story and he just said it was the power of my mind that did that. My mind conjured up something about a kneecap and the next day sent electricity to someone I had never seen who just happened to be in the audience and his infection was healed? His interpretation takes faith, it seems to me. The interpretation and grid we look through, as was true with Jesus' miracles, is always at play. And as Jesus said, for someone who is just against believing, even if a person came back from the dead, it would still not make them believe (Luke 16:31).

But as for me, I am like the blind man whom He healed and came back unable to explain it, but said, "But I know this: I was blind, and now I can see!" (John 9:25 NLT). I can't explain it all, either, but I have known miracles in my life.

Many miracles are taking place today in the Muslim world, as Jesus is appearing to Muslims all over the world and telling them He is real and is, to use the term my friend used, "true-true." He is the true God. For several years I have followed this movement and books have been written on it. One of the most fascinating events I know of firsthand is a man who was raised as a terrorist in the Middle East and had been participating in jihad since his youth. In his twenties he moved to the US to recruit young US Muslim men into jihad. After being here for a few weeks, he had a bad car accident, and while he was recuperating, he began to doubt his faith in Allah and was praying asking Allah if he was the real God or not. As he was praying, he said that Jesus appeared to him and called him to follow Him . . . telling him *He* was the real God. As he described it, it was undeniable, and he left his Muslim faith and life of terrorism and now works in a ministry to reconcile Jews and Muslims.

And close to my heart, since I have so many Jewish friends whom I love deeply, are many miraculous stories of people who are called Messianic Jews, Jewish people who have come to believe that Jesus is the Jewish messiah as He said He was. I love hearing and reading the miraculous interventions in their lives that bring them to faith in Jesus, as it is one more piece of evidence that Jesus is very much alive today and still calling Jewish people to Himself. I am often surprised also at how many of my Jewish friends do not know either the Old Testament prophecies that He fulfilled, that He was a rabbi, teaching in the temple, etc. Or that the Christian faith began with His Jewish followers, and that the New Testament was written by Jews. Also, I love to tell them to read Isaiah 53 from their Bible, what we call the Old Testament . . . a very direct picture of the coming Messiah being crucified. Written thousands of years ago, way before Jesus, it describes Jesus and his suffering perfectly.

In summary, apart from my own experiences, I became satisfied through a lot of research that the miracles of the Bible not only happened in the past but are still happening today.

THE MOST IMPORTANT FACT IN THE BIBLE

The singular most important fact in the Bible is also the biggest hurdle for many people: the resurrection of Jesus.

And, frankly, it should be the big question to be answered, as the Bible itself says, if Christ's resurrection did not happen, then we more than all people, are to be pitied. More directly, it says, "And if Christ has not been raised, our preaching is worthless, and so is your faith" (1 Corinthians 15:14 BSB). The apostle Paul said directly that if this were not true, not only were he and the rest of them liars, but the whole faith is worth nothing. Said another way, the entire truth of Christianity rests on the resurrection of Jesus. Speaking to the people of Athens, Paul the apostle said this:

> ***In the past God overlooked such ignorance [referring to idol worship], but now he commands all people everywhere to repent. For he has set a day when he will judge the world with justice by the man he has appointed. He has given proof of this to everyone by raising him from the dead.*** (Acts 17: 30–31)

The entire New Testament's message about who Jesus is rests upon one question: did he "true-true" rise from the dead? If He did, then it proves that He was the Messiah, and if He didn't, then as Paul said, we are to be the most pitied of all people . . . following a faith based on a fairy tale. But Paul, having experienced Jesus in his radical conversion on the Damascus Road, had no doubt, so much so that he spent the rest of his life traveling throughout that world proclaiming the gospel of Jesus, even when being beaten, persecuted, imprisoned and finally killed. And, as he wrote to the Romans, his message was the same simple one that the entire early believers shared, the "message concerning faith that we proclaim" (Romans 10:8):

> ***If you declare with your mouth, 'Jesus is Lord,' and believe in your heart that God raised him***

> ***from the dead, you will be saved. For it is with your heart that you believe and are justified, and it is with your mouth that you profess your faith and are saved.*** (Romans 10:9–10)

Throughout the New Testament, the resurrection is the front and center issue, as it not only showed that Jesus was the Messiah, but also validated that He had accomplished His mission of overcoming death itself, both spiritual and physical.

So, the evidence for the resurrection is paramount. As I mentioned earlier, I had been convinced that He was alive because of my experience. But later, in the season of looking at the objections people had to the faith, I also began to look at the evidence.

You can't have a resurrection without a death. His crucifixion and death were attested to not only by the Bible but also by secular historians and writers. Josephus, Tacitus, Lucian, and the Jewish Talmud all write about his crucifixion. The Bible consistently refers to it and to the testimonies of those who were there and knew about it.

There is no account in history of anyone ever surviving a Roman crucifixion. No one disputes that he was crucified, but some try to say that he was really not dead. But there is no account anywhere to say that he was not, and no one has ever survived that crucifixion. He was, in fact, dead.

DEAD MAN GONE: THE TOMB WAS EMPTY

The accounts of what happened on that first Easter morning are sound. The tomb had been sealed and guarded, and yet . . . He was gone. Grave clothes left in place. If you study how prepared and equipped the soldiers and guards would have been to protect that grave, you know they did not just let him sneak out . . . much less help him roll away the stone. It was all very secure.

And even the opponents of the empty tomb agreed that it was empty . . . they said "the disciples stole the body."

Testimony, Behavior, and the Fate of the Eyewitnesses

There were many eyewitnesses to not only Jesus' life, but also to His appearances after the resurrection. Not only His disciples, but other followers and also the authors of New Testament books, as well as sources outside the New Testament, attest to the resurrection. And witnesses attest to his appearing to over five hundred people.

These witnesses continued in their testimony and turned into bold evangelists, ready to do anything to tell others about this risen Christ. The movement began to spread because of them.

They continued in this message, even though they were persecuted and many were killed because of their testimony. Those deaths are written about by extrabiblical writers as well. It is hard to believe that so many people would die for what they knew was a lie. I am sure someone would have finally given in and said, "Okay, just kidding, if you are going to kill me." But they kept on, right to their deaths. But they did not die for a lie . . . they died because they knew that He had risen from the dead. We also have a creed of the early church written within months of his resurrection, attesting to that resurrection *by the ones who were in fact there.*

In examining the historical evidence that what the Bible says about the resurrection, I came to the conclusion that what I was experiencing was not only true for me, but it was "true-true" history. This cognitive dissonance for me was settled. And in the years since, I can continue to attest through my own experience, He is alive. He was, in fact, raised.

Ten

Jesus, Please Explain Your Followers

There were some of the obstacles to faith I had from the "evidence" columns. Those questions were settled for me through study. Data. Facts.

But there were a couple of other obstacles that I had to get around as well: the pain and suffering of life, and some Christians. Here is what I learned that helped me understand those Christians who make us doubt.

A number of years ago, we had a new family move in next door to us. It was an instant connection . . . we both had new baby girls, the husband and I had both just begun new businesses, so we were in the same phases of life. I was glad they had moved in.

After a few weeks of just chatting here and there, we invited them over for dinner and looked forward to going a bit deeper in knowing more about them and their lives. It was a fun time of getting to know them.

At some point, I asked the wife about her family, and she began to tell us all about where she grew up and her parents and siblings. Then all of a sudden her demeanor totally changed . . . as she shifted from talking about one of her sisters to another. She said, "And then . . . also . . . I have one sister who is one of those crazy Christians. You know . . . the 'born again' type. That stuff drives me nuts!"

I nodded, and just said, "Yeah . . . I know what you mean."

"So you know some of them too?" she asked.

"Oh, yeah. I know lots of them," I replied, and then she returned to more accounts of her experiences with "crazy Christians" in her life. (Note to self at that moment . . . I might want to not talk too much about my faith for a while . . . that probably won't go well.)

As she shared, I couldn't help but agree with much of what she said about some of the things she had seen some Christians do and some of the experiences she had had with them. They ranged from stupid, to more stupid, to outright hurtful. I felt embarrassed. But I think the thing that stood out to me most about that conversation was the crappy bind that I felt like I was in. I would love to be able to talk about my faith with her—or anyone else. I want to share the love and reality of God with others. But the crappy feeling was that I couldn't do that, because she had already developed a view of what a Christian was and what it meant to be one. I knew anything I had to say was not going to put much of a dent in that view. I would just suddenly be "one of those" nutcases, in her view. So, the dinner continued, and our friendship developed along a path that did not include many discussions about faith for quite a while. That was fine . . . we liked them and had a lot of fun and meaningful times with them as our relationship developed.

To be honest, I feel that way a lot. I often want to talk about God and how great I have found Him to be . . . and yet I know the person I am talking to might, or probably does, already have a box I will be put in. As my friend who I wrote about in the preface said, "Oh . . . he is one of those."

Because the sad reality is that many of those views are learned for very good reason.

People have sometimes been hurt by a Christian or a church, maybe severely. They have known hypocrites. They have been lied to or swindled, or just seen a "Christian" who was worse than unlikable and maybe even mean in some way.

My Jewish friend I wrote about before—the one who was afraid I was going to try to "convert" him and that I was "one of those" Christian types—sent me an email about what had just happened to him:

> *We were at Lake X with another couple [who are also Jewish], and we hired a kid to take us water-skiing on his boat. It got hot, he took off his shirt, and he had an enormous crucifix tattoo across his back. My friend commented on it (I mean, it was hard not to notice!), and the kid said, "What's your relationship to Jesus?" We were like, dude, we're here to water-ski, and we're Jewish. Wrong crowd, wrong time, and wrong question, since not everyone believes Jesus is God. But he was young and enthusiastic.*
>
> *A couple hours later, the boat broke. Totally lost power and wouldn't start. He had to call someone to come tow us to the marina. A boat eventually showed up, and as they were tying a tow rope to the boat, I noticed the kid looking down at that little emergency safety clip—you probably know what it's called—the thing that you can attach to your lifejacket so if you go overboard the boat stops. The kid gave it a little jimmy, it clicked in, and the boat restarted. He made a big deal about the battery working, maybe it had charged up, etc., but he didn't say, "Guys, I'm really sorry. I'd accidentally knocked the kill switch loose." It was a WWJD moment—would Jesus have covered up a mistake like this? My point being, as hard as it must be to get a large crucifix*

tattooed on your back, it's even harder to embody the principles that symbol represents in your day-to-day life.

What a great example of this kind of experience that so many people have had.

Think of having a parent who talks about God but then treats you like crap. Or worse, a pastor or youth worker or priest who molests you. Or a husband who claims the name of Jesus and is abusive. Sadly, what we know of God is certainly influenced by who we know of God.

I would love for my friends and others to know my faith experience, not just their experience of people who have hurt them or not been good to them in their past. And there are other people who I would like to really know me as I really am, and my faith as it really is, with whom that will never happen because of Christians who have given them crummy experiences.

I was under contract to speak at a secular worldwide leadership event, broadcasted to arenas. Many of the biggest companies in the world would be attending, and I had spoken there several times before. The arena in this particular city was controlled by city permits, and because someone on the city council associated me with someone else's "Christian" views, they not only banned *me*, but would not allow the *event* to take place in their arena because I was "one of those." I never found out specifically what happened, but apparently, someone on that city's leadership council had had some negative experiences with Christians that tainted their view of what I was going to be like. Guilt by association.

There is another aspect to this problem that is particularly troubling: the damage that poorly behaving Christians' behavior does to God's reputation. After all, He is the One who is getting judged here as someone not worth knowing because of how someone who has carried His name has behaved. Everyone loses. Here is how the apostle Paul expressed it:

> ***Do not become a stumbling block, whether to Jews or Greeks or the church of God—as I also try to please everyone in all I do. For I am not seeking my own good, but the good of many, that they may be saved.*** (1 Corinthians 10:32–33 bsb)

God doesn't want anyone getting in the way of your being able to see Him for who He is, and if that has ever happened to you, I am sorry. Give Him another chance.

WHAT HELPED ME

So, when I entered this new life of faith, I came in with many of the same experiences and tainted views. But as I studied, I began to understand that the Christianity I had problems with was not real Christianity at all. It was how I had seen it lived out by religious people who apparently had never read much of the Bible. It seemed that the ones who kind of held themselves out to be the "spiritual" ones above everyone else were the very types that were on the receiving end of God's anger in more than one occasion in Scripture! I was relieved. As I read God's words, I understood that He was not like those people at all. So, this really helped me overcome many of those objections to faith that were hanging out in my head.

For one, I did not have to be weird to be a Christian. I could still have a beer or a glass of wine . . . it said so right in the Bible! (I was really amazed to see that there, in multiple places.)

Also, I did not have to go be a minister or a missionary in Africa . . . I could have a normal profession, and God would still be pleased with my work. He invented our work. It said so right in the Bible! And what seemed like a thousand other things as well were right there in the Bible, which made it all make sense, particularly about some of the more hurtful things that happen at the hands of Christians or churches.

JUDGMENTAL CHRISTIANS

I was talking to a contractor who does work for our company and he was telling me about growing up around a particular church where the youth group had a big presence in his neighborhood. He said that after being around them, he didn't want anything to do with church or God, as they were always telling him how "bad" he was. We all probably can relate to that feeling of being looked down upon by self-righteous religious people. There is something about humans that allows us to mistake religiosity for spirituality. Religiosity inevitably leads to judgment and worrying about who is good and who is bad.

Christians aren't the only people who do this. I had a producer from one of the Hollywood studios I was working with, who was a New Ager, not a Christian, ask me how I was one time. It was right after my mother, my father, and my brother-in-law had all died suddenly within weeks of one another. I told him it had been a tough couple of months for me dealing with losing all three of them so quickly.

He responded with "Well, you should really take a look at how and why you are attracting all of this death into your life."

I was stunned. I had no response. I had heard guilt messages before, as a person and as a psychologist, but that one took the cake. According to him, the "law of attraction" was responsible for their deaths, and I did it? I just shook my head and moved on.

But Jesus didn't just shake his head and move on when people, and even His people, were judgmental of others. There is so much to say about this topic, but I want to begin with this: if you think Christianity is judgmental, then you have been misled by someone. Judgment was *not* Jesus, nor his message. Yet, I am surprised how many people feel like guilt is one of the main tenets of Christianity.

We moved to a new neighborhood when our daughters were just born, and one Sunday morning I was loading them into the car when my neighbor said, "Morning . . . where are y'all headed?"

"Church," I replied. "Want to come?"

"Are you kidding?" she said. "No way."

"How come?"

"I can't take the guilt!"

I wished I was not in a hurry, as I would have loved to unpack that one. But I do remember thinking, *How did a faith whose founder, Jesus, literally came to end guilt forever with a message of forgiveness become the Walmart of selling guilt?*

Seriously! Listen to what Jesus said:

> ***For I did not come to judge the world, but to save the world.*** (John 12:47)

Over and over He stood against those religious people who judged others. Once, when a woman was caught in adultery and the church leaders brought her to Jesus to be judged, saying she should be stoned, He turned to them and said, "Let any one of you who is without sin be the first to throw a stone at her" (John 8:7).

Jesus also said:

> ***Do not judge, and you will not be judged. Do not condemn, and you will not be condemned. Forgive, and you will be forgiven.*** (Luke 6:37)

> ***Why do you look at the speck in your brother's eye, but fail to notice the beam in your own eye? How can you say to your brother, "Let me take the speck out of your eye," while there is still a beam in your own eye? You hypocrite! First take the beam out of your own eye, and then you will see clearly to remove the speck from your brother's eye.*** (Matthew 7:3–5 BSB)

We see plentiful examples in Scripture where the judgmental are blasted:

> ***Those who are pure in their own eyes and yet are not cleansed of their filth; those whose eyes are ever so haughty, whose glances are so disdainful.*** (Proverbs 30:12–13)
>
> ***You, therefore, have no excuse, you who pass judgment on someone else, for at whatever point you judge another, you are condemning yourself, because you who pass judgment do the same things.*** (Romans 2:1)

Going around judging or condemning people was not what He did, other than condemning the condemnation of the "condemning people," the "hypocrites" as He called them. He did point out bad behavior . . . and He told us to do that as well. But that is what we all desire from our friends, right? I mean, if you have a friend caught up in a destructive pattern, you would hopefully intervene—into an addiction that might kill them, an attitude that is destroying their marriage, or a behavior that might cause them to lose their job. That is what friends do. But there is a huge difference in being honest with one another to stop destructive behavior versus judging or condemning.

The Bible tells us when we do point out destructive behavior, to do it with "gentleness and humility . . . examining oneself first" . . . "getting the log out of our own eye" realizing we are no better than the one we are helping—that is curative, and it is what God calls Christians to. This is what you pay a good psychologist to do . . . tell you where you can do better without making you feel like crap.

Jesus already knows that we are all imperfect, and we are already "guilty" of breaking God's perfect laws. He was clear about how dysfunctional we all are. Who has not lied? Or lusted? Or been envious, coveting another person in some way? Or behaved in some way that you wish you could take back? Or been overcome by anger, resentment, or unforgiveness at some time or another? We all have, and we know it (unless someone is an extreme narcissist and in massive denial of their own stuff). Jesus approaches all of us, knowing we are guilty of lots of things, and he came into the world with the message: forgiveness to all. Free. No condemnation. All you have to do is accept it.

It really helped me to know that this is the real faith, and not the judgmental ones or the hypocrites. The faith does not support any of that kind of behavior.

THE HYPOCRITES

How about "Christians" who do really bad and hurtful things, or even really fail at times to live up to the standards that the Bible speaks of, while they go about claiming a faith or even bragging about it? How can that be? Why are some Christians so bad, or many Christians bad at least some time or another?

Said another way, if the faith is supposed to help us become more loving, honest, and better people, how then can it be "true-true" and we still see Christians who are not loving, honest, or better people, all the while claiming Jesus? How can they have a crucifix tattooed on their back, as my friend said, and be intrusive, and fail you, and then lie about their behavior?

Doesn't that negate the reality of the faith?

Good question.

Remember when I said that God has a marketing problem? He is selling something: Himself. But in the sales brochure, He tells us that you will look at His "church," and it will be a *very* mixed bag. He is not selling a perfect resort package, where everything looks great, including the church itself. After all, by definition, the membership requirement is to be a sinner. That is the badge that gets one in the door. And he also says that some will come into the door who are intruders or imposters.

Here is just some of what He says about the bad behavior He promises you will see from those who call themselves "Christians."

First, he gives us an overall warning. The "bad guys" will be there, in church, and people will ask "Why do You allow that?" When asked about rooting all the "bad" ones out so only the "good ones" are there, He said this:

> ***"No," he said, "if you pull the weeds now, you might uproot the wheat with them. Let both grow together until the harvest. At that time I will tell the harvesters: First collect the weeds and tie them in bundles to be burned; then gather the wheat into my barn."***
>
> (Matthew 13:29–30 BSB)

And then, He promised some really bad things were in store for the "weeds":

> ***Likewise, every good tree bears good fruit, but a bad tree bears bad fruit. A good tree cannot bear bad fruit, and a bad tree cannot bear good fruit. Every tree that does not bear good fruit is cut down and thrown into the fire. So then, by their fruit you will recognize them. Not everyone who says to Me, "Lord, Lord," will enter the kingdom of heaven, but only he who does the will of My Father in heaven. Many will say to Me on that day, "Lord, Lord, did we not prophesy in Your name, and in Your name drive out demons and perform many miracles?" Then I will tell them plainly, "I never knew you; depart from Me, you workers of lawlessness!"*** (Matthew 7:17–23 BSB)

The Bible is clear, and He was clear, that just because someone claims to be a person of faith does not mean they are the real thing. And, worse, He allows them to continue to invade the household of faith for a while and live there while He is gathering the entire group who does want to follow Him in truth. He doesn't want to "uproot" the baby with the bathwater.

There are false teachers who are in it for power and money (see Matthew 23:14, 2 Peter 2:2–3), and the Bible actually says what you are saying yourself, which is that their behavior will make the faith look bad—literally, it will be "defamed." You will know them by their fruits—their behavior—and it will defame the church. We see that all the time. Ouch.

> ***Many will follow in their depravity, and because of them the way of truth will be defamed. In***

> ***their greed, these false teachers will exploit you with deceptive words. The longstanding verdict against them remains in force, and their destruction does not sleep.*** (2 Peter 2:2–3 BSB)

Nor will the mean people who call themselves Christians and yet are behaving really badly as a life pattern or are not loving be able to stand in the end. The Bible says it clearly:

> ***This is how we know who the children of God are and who the children of the devil are: Anyone who does not do what is right is not God's child, nor is anyone who does not love their brother and sister. Anyone who does not love remains in death. Anyone who hates a brother or sister is a murderer, and you know that no murderer has eternal life residing in him.*** (1 John 3:10, 14–15)

Bottom line: do not be surprised by bad, unloving people in the church, but *expect* it. He *told* us they would be there. And He also said to learn to recognize them.

NOT BLACK AND WHITE

Here is another confusing issue: some people are truly people of faith, and yet fail horribly. The Bible is clear that none of us is perfect or is without sin. Even David, a man "after God's own heart," seduced someone else's wife, and then had the husband killed. That is truly horrible behavior . . . yet he really was the "real thing" over the long haul. Afterward he was sorry, repented and sought forgiveness, but it is true that he really did some terrible things.

Other people get caught up in the worries, pleasures, and riches of this life and do not become fruitful. ("Fruit" in the Bible describes such things as love, kindness, faithfulness, and other behavior we all desire.) Addictions, materialism, narcissism, and greed are good examples of being "caught up" in the dysfunction of this world. Some people are really immature and focus on the wrong things. Here is one description of some people that Jesus gave:

> ***But all too quickly the message is crowded out by the worries of this life, the lure of wealth, and the desire for other things, so no fruit is produced.*** (Mark 4:19 NLT)

Some people are so driven by greed or their addiction to a shallow, materialistic life or prideful image or narcissistic advancement, they are really not behaving well, and not being "fruitful," as the Bible puts it. Because of these pursuits, they are neglecting their spiritual growth. Others have "backslidden" for a season, as the passage above said, and are "caught up in a trespass." I have treated countless people of real faith who have been "caught up" in an addiction, or an affair, or some other pattern of destructive behavior. But, they were not forever happy, remaining in denial . . . at some point they became remorseful and turned around. And then there are others, as the Bible says, who "were never really part of us" (1 John 2:19 GW). Some were faking it the whole time. Some people who are failing are the real thing, caught up in a pattern of immaturity, and others are not real at all, even though they claim the "Name."

The standard is not perfection, as any of us would fail and be voted off the island. But God is patient with anyone who truly wants to be in relationship with Him and get better, even when we find it hard to share that patience and grace. And forget the more heinous sins for a moment. What about all of us and our ongoing immature dysfunctional patterns that hurt our lives or relationships? Defensiveness? Selfishness? Greed? Lust? Pride? We all have it, this imperfection called sin. The Bible is clear that there is no one who never sins, even a righteous person (Ecclesiastes 7:20). Or as John puts it,

> ***If we say that we have no sin, we deceive ourselves, and the truth is not in us. If we confess our sins, He is faithful and just to forgive us our sins and to cleanse us from all unrighteousness. If we say we have not sinned, we make Him out to be a liar, and His word is not in us.*** (1 John 1:8–10 NKJV)

So, first of all, there are people who claim to be good, who do hurtful things, claim to be Christian and hang out in the church, but are not really Christian, even if they say they are. And second, there are real Christians who fail. To various degrees, all of us fail. Some fall harder, further, uglier, and longer than others, but we all fall short in some ways at some times. And God has grace for that.

Sometimes people are struggling with their own behavior, not wanting to be doing what they are doing, but finding it difficult to change. But, if they are the real thing, usually they will at some point turn around when the "pleasure time" runs its course or hopefully, they hit bottom or are awakened. As Peter, the apostle, says, "As a result, they do not live the rest of their earthly lives for evil human desires, but rather for the will of God. For you have spent enough time in the past doing what pagans choose to do—living in debauchery, lust, drunkenness, orgies, carousing and detestable idolatry" (1 Peter 4:2–3 NIV). Said another way, Hey guys . . . you are supposed to be living a bit better than this, as God wants you to. Time's up, get sober! Grow up!" At some point, you usually find out how true someone is by their eventual unhappiness with patterns of bad behavior and they begin to exhibit a desire to change, Imperfect as they may be. And God always welcomes them with grace and forgiveness. Even if they are being caught up in the worries, riches, or pleasures of this life and are immature or totally lost. So, don't be surprised when you see it, or even if you find some time that you are being that way. God will always be there ready to forgive if you turn to Him. But do not judge Jesus as being false by the bad behavior of people that He himself told us would be in the "camp."

TRUE BELIEVERS

There really are many very good Christians out there. I am amazed over and over at how many there are and how amazing they are. Truly loving, truly giving, truly honest and responsible. *So* many of them. That is the third group . . . the "mature" ones, as the Bible calls them, who bear "good fruit." And if you want to know how to appropriately and accurately evaluate what a true biblical faith is, here is just a little sample of some of the ways the Bible describes the real thing, and what to look for:

> ***Pure and undefiled religion before our God and Father is this: to care for orphans and widows in their distress, and to keep oneself from being polluted by the world.*** (James 1:27 BSB)
>
> ***Do not oppress widows, orphans, foreigners, and the poor. And do not scheme against each other.*** (Zechariah 7:10 nlt)

> ***Then the King will say to those on His right, "Come, you who are blessed by My Father, inherit the kingdom prepared for you from the foundation of the world. For I was hungry and you gave Me something to eat, I was thirsty and you gave Me something to drink, I was a stranger and you took Me in, I was naked and you clothed Me, I was sick and you looked after Me, I was in prison and you visited Me." Then the righteous will answer Him, "Lord, when did we see You hungry and feed You, or thirsty and give You something to drink? When did we see You a stranger and take You in, or naked and clothe You? When did we see You sick or in prison and visit You?" And the King will reply, "Truly I tell you, whatever you did for one of the least of these brothers of Mine, you did for Me."*** (Matthew 25:34–40 BSB)

In another place, God describes what the real thing looks like:

> ***Isn't it to share your bread with the hungry, to bring the poor and homeless into your home, to clothe the naked when you see him, and not to turn away from your own flesh and blood?*** (Isaiah 58:7 BSB)

The acts of the flesh are obvious: sexual immorality, impurity, and debauchery; idolatry and sorcery; hatred, discord, jealousy, and rage; rivalries, divisions, factions, and envy; drunkenness, orgies, and the like. I warn you, as I did before, that those who practice such things will not inherit the kingdom of God.

> ***But the fruit of the Spirit is love, joy, peace, patience, kindness, goodness, faithfulness, gentleness, and self-control. Against such things there is no law.*** (Galatians 5:22–23)

Compare the people you know who are like the first list versus the ones who are like the second list. True faith is not hard to spot.

I had a friend who was listing all of her objections to the faith, because of the bad behavior of some, which were exactly the ones I have written about here that I objected to also. I said, "Good news! The Bible agrees with you! And not only that, you agree with it, too, about what the good things in life are!"

"Like what?" she said.

"Well, like the stuff you care about: love, responsibility, freedom, honesty, justice, compassion, forgiveness, second chances, developing and using your talents, having purpose, relationships, giving, parties and celebrations, family, deep friendships . . . That's pretty much what the whole book is about. That is what the Bible says God wants us to be like. You sound like a Christian and don't even know it!" I laughed.

We laughed, but there is a truth there. When loving and responsible people begin to see what the Bible really says, they find that it is against most of the things they are against and that it is for the things they love. You want Christians to be good, and so does He. Just don't be surprised sometimes when they are not (or the fakes who claim to be), because He warned us that would happen. It in no way negates the message of the Bible. In fact, it supports it.

Eleven

The Greatest Obstacle of All

MY HARDEST OBJECTION: HOW CAN A GOOD GOD ALLOW SUFFERING AND EVIL?

In one sense, at least for me, God was easy to believe in. All I had to do was look at the sky at night or read a neurology book. And, at the same time, some facts made it hard to believe, like "Why were some Christians and churches so mean?" So the path of faith was one of no questions sometimes and lots of questions at other times. We have looked at many of those.

But for me, there is one obstacle that rises way above all of the rest as the most difficult, and although there is a very credible, believable, and more than intellectually satisfactory answer for me, I still have trouble stomaching it. And it is this: If God is loving and good and all-powerful and could end all suffering, why do we have it? How can a loving God allow this to go on? Where is He??

For me, that is the really, really (really) hard one. To believe in a God who can look at all of the suffering in the world and not seem to do more at times. For the innocent, and for the good people to whom horrible things happen . . . Why, God? Why? It makes no sense.

I have lost many people I have loved in my life, beginning in early childhood. I grew too familiar with death too early. But I learned to deal with it and coped and have not been overly scarred. I learned that it was a part of life, painful as it was. It did not make me question God for some reason.

But there was one that I just could not really ever metabolize and fit it into some box I could live with. I had very close friends who lost their son to a rare childhood cancer. I was very close to him and they are like family to me. He was young, talented, gifted, loving, a person of faith, and had an incredible future in front of him. I could not stand it that he got sick and died. It was too much.

And part of it that made it too much was the injustice of it all . . . not only for him but also his parents. I have never known better people, with better hearts whose entire life and career was totally spent on serving and helping others. Not to idealize, but they are just as good as humans can get. And something got to me so deep about how while no one deserves this, they *especially* did not deserve this. Here they are, living a lifetime of sacrifice and service to others, and this is what they get. And their lives are 100 percent about serving God and others in the ministry. I just could not make it work, and I still can't totally get my head around it. Even though the grief heals, resolution comes, and we have all gone on with life having great memories of him . . . and laugh and cherish his life when we are together. We celebrate him. We are okay.

But still, the question is still not fully answered for me: God, how could You allow this to happen to someone so good?

I could not find an answer to that question, in the very least, emotionally, and still don't have one.

Why do we have genocide, or senseless wars? Why abuse in families? Why child trafficking? It is often too much to get my head around, how God allows all of that to go on. Maybe you have had that same experience. Someone you have lost, or some tragedy that befell you or someone you love. Or maybe you have had a life not touched by tragedy yourself, but when you read the papers or listen to the news, as a compassionate person, you are far too aware of all of the evil and the suffering in the world to not have the same question emerge in your own heart and mind. And to me, it remains the hardest one. The assumption that most of us make is that if God were really good and compassionate, and truly all powerful, He would get rid of all of the pain and suffering in the world. He would certainly do more than it seems He often does.

So, what helped me deal with this one? An answer that doesn't resolve every question and wondering, as there is still some ongoing mystery, but one that is intellectually and spiritually honest and secure to stand firm while still having questions.

Ironically, the answer I was looking for was found in the love of God. The very thing that I was doubting is where I found the answer. Suffering does not mean that God loves us less. It actually points to how crazy, how big, and how huge He loves us. God's love for us is so great that He gives us freedom. And when you study the problem of evil, suffering, and a good God, I have come to understand a reality that I can accept. It is the reality of what love requires to exist:

Freedom.

He loves us so much that He gave us freedom, so that love could be real. God created the earth for humans and to have a relationship with humans based on love. He wanted to love us, and He wanted us to love Him.

And He loved us so much He wanted to entrust His entire creation to us, to be His "image bearers" on earth. Said another way, we were to do on earth what God would do if He were the one doing it. He made us to take care of it all. He turned it over to us. We, humans, are his "crown of creation," the Bible says:

> ***You have made them a little lower than the angels and crowned them with glory and honor. You made them rulers over the works of your hands; you put everything under their feet: all flocks and herds, and the animals of the wild, the birds in the sky, and the fish in the sea, all that swim the paths of the seas.*** (Psalm 8:5–8)

He loves us. And He wants us to love Him back. In fact, the entire Bible can be seen as a love story between God, mankind, and His other created beings. A romance that started out great and was broken by our rejection of God. Humans rejected Him.

But it was not supposed to be that way. God loved us and designed us to love Him, but love embodies something else in order to truly exist, and that is freedom. Freedom of choice. Let's look at how.

FREEDOM

If we are not free, if we do not have true free will and choice, we cannot have love. You know this if you have ever been manipulated into loving someone the way they demanded to be loved. They used guilt, leverage, or some other control mechanism to get you to do what they want you to do. If we are controlled in a relationship and love someone or do what they want only because we have to and have no choice, that is no longer love. It is slavery. We are not free. Marriages break up all of the time because of one spouse trying to control the other. Kids develop mental health issues and rebel often as a result of controlling parents who do not allow freedom of choice within boundaries. Freedom is essential to all of life's thriving, but particularly for love to thrive. Psychologists will tell you that the height of romantic love, sexual performance and orgasmic functioning, is diminished when someone feels controlled by their partner. Or under some controlling performance anxiety in order to feel accepted, to feel loved. Freedom is essential for love to exist. God did not want to receive "love" from us if we were robots who had to love and obey Him, with no choice. People who did not have the choice to not love Him. He wanted the real thing.

So, God set us free when He created us. He gave us 100 percent real and total freedom to love Him and obey Him or, equally, to turn from Him and break the relationship. He also gave us 100 percent trust. He trusted us to run the earth. He trusted us to love not only Him but each other. He trusted us to not pollute the earth but to nurture it and care for it, as well as all of the Creation. To use all He has given us to be fruitful in all our endeavors, work, and relationships. It was a serious act of love . . . to give us all of this, and set us free to either take care of it and love Him back, or turn against Him and reject Him. He laid it all on the line.

Now, he did have another option. He could have created us to be robots with no free will. He could have a remote control and make us love Him and make us do everything He wanted. But that would not be freedom. It would not be free will. And as a result, there could not have been real love. But He did not set it up that way, making us little robotic toys, like we build today, that do whatever we push a button to have them do. He set us free instead.

But . . . freedom also means real consequences. We were free to turn against Him, but there would be consequences if we chose another path. He said it plainly: "If you eat of the tree of the knowledge of good and evil, you will die" (see Genesis 2:16). We were *never* supposed to know the experience of both good and evil. We were supposed to live in an ideal life, like we all long for.

So, God told us clearly with a warning of the consequences. Said another way: "if you unplug from Life (Me) and try to be Life unto yourself, to be your own God, you will die. When you unplug from Life you will be lost in the ongoing experience of death." To be separated from Life *is* death. Think about that. It is a truism. God is life, and to separate ourselves from Life (Him) is by definition "Death." I am a scuba diver, and if I unplug from my air tank, I will die. I have a choice, but there are consequences, as there is no life without air. And as God said, there is no "life" without the One who is "Life."

But He did give us the freedom to do that . . . and we did. So now we have this experience of experiencing "death" in the creation, every day. In relationships, in the world around us, in governments, families, our bodies, and every aspect of creation. All of our existence, as good as it can be sometimes, is marred by this disease called death, which is separation from God.

Unplug the light from the power source, and the lights go out. Period. And that is what happened. We left the One from whom all goodness comes, and only goodness . . . and now we were in charge of the earth, trying to play the role of God, but without the fullness of Life that only He is the source of. And now, the life that we do have has been infected with the disease of death, and death processes. In ourselves, our bodies, our relationships and everything else. You see the beauty of the creation or of a person, but pain and badness alongside the goodness of it all to various degrees.

This was not hard for me, as a psychologist, to understand. We have all seen it. A baby derives life from her source, her mother, from conception. For nine months, she is connected to "life" and gets everything she needs in utero from her mother. Then, one day, it happens. The baby is born, and for the first time, the experience of the "knowledge of good and evil" happens. The moment she is separated from "life" and is "out there on her own," even in the first few seconds, you see the "weeping and gnashing of teeth" on her face. The very picture Jesus used to describe hell. Weeping, screaming, gnashing. You can see hell on the face of a screaming infant. Separation from life *is* hell. It *is* death.

That is exactly what happened to us at the Fall of mankind. However you interpret Genesis in terms of how and when the truth of the drama occurred, one truth is told: humans were tempted by the tempter to do life on their own by turning from God. Humanity snipped the cord and is no longer connected to Him. And death, meaning everything that is not God, entered the world and infected the goodness of us and the goodness of the Creation: Now we have control and not freedom in relationships. Meanness and not compassion. Murder of people's souls and even bodies and not looking out for one another's good. Envy, greed, pride, narcissism, lying, cheating, and more. Disease and not health. And on and on. We separated from Life and got death, just as He said we would. This is not difficult for us to see before our eyes every day . . . just listen to the news. As He said, "Do not eat of that tree or you will die." We see the "death" of many good things all the time.

So, God loved us so much to give us freedom, and we chose against Him. We ran away from home. And it did not work out well at all. Today, that is the world that we live in.

Another analogy. As a psychologist, I am very troubled when I see "helicopter" parenting. It hurts children's development. They need to be free to grow, choose, even if that freedom is risky, and they fall down and hurt themselves, because they then learn to not fall down! Freedom, even in this fallen world, is required to be all they were designed to be, even if there is risk to letting them walk. That is the good side of the risk of freedom . . . No falling down, no learning to walk as a toddler. In fact, the average toddler falls seventeen times per hour! But if you took all of their steps for them, and never let them go, they would never learn to walk.[1] You have to give kids freedom to be all that they can be.

So, if you are a parent, you do what God did. You give them freedom to be themselves, and you do not stand there turning them into little overcontrolled robots. You send them into the playground to play on their own. And, like God did in the Creation, you give them the rules: You say, "Stay in the yard, don't hit each other, stay out of the thorny bushes," etc. Or, if they are older, "Don't believe the tempter [dealer)] who says the drugs are good and won't hurt you." "Make good choices" is something most parents say as they begin to "let go" and give freedom. If they obey you, they will be fine. When they tell their kids, "Do not eat of that tree! Or you will suffer," this is not a bad analogy to what God did with us. If they obey your big rules and don't eat of the trees that bring death, they will be fine. "Play kickball, but don't run into the street." Freedom *within* boundaries.

But if you are a parent really scared of freedom and all of its risks . . . you can take away their freedom and shadow them and make all of their choices for them. You could control their very steps to make sure they never say yes to a drug dealer, or get in a conflict or prevent whatever bad consequence you wanted to control them out of, to protect them. You could prevent their drug use, but, if you did that, *they would cease to be human*. They are just your little robots at that point. Instead, you want them to voluntarily stay "faithful" to your command to "not eat of that tree," and thrive.

God was not willing to make robots. He loves us. He is a loving parent. He wanted humans to love. And to be human, to be in His image, you *have to be free*. Free to follow Him and stay connected to all that is good and alive, or separate from Him and Life and experience the pain of "knowing good and evil." You want your kids to be nice to their playmates or siblings, and enjoy the fun they can have together. But, they could also turn against all you said and not be nice to their sister and instead, hit her, or worse. Or they could run into the street you told them to not go into . . . or strangle the dog or even climb over the fence and land in a neighboring forest of scary dangers. When a child unplugs from good parents and goes their own way, *things do not go well*. And there are very real consequences, but real consequences that every parent must afford their children to choose if they are going to give them the freedom to thrive, and if they really love their children well.

I have daughters who learned to drive . . . and I had to trust them to be able to take the cars and not drink and drive, as some high schoolers might do. I had to give them that freedom if they were going to be fully human and develop. But, they could have made disastrous choices with disastrous consequences as a result of that freedom. Every parent knows that risk. It is the price of freedom. *And as such, it is the price of love*. It holds an incredible upside, and disastrous possible downsides.

And He gave us that freedom, and we used it to turn against Him and now we live in a world that was created to be good, but has gone bad because of the choice of the human race to unplug from God. Creation still retains the good . . . there is love, and all the good things are still here, but it is all subject to also being diseased in the same world, or in the same person. The good coexists with evil in the world and is tainted by it, sometimes a little, and sometimes all the way. We know what a little badness mixed into a good person can look like and how it can spoil an evening, and we also know what pure evil looks like in some other circumstances. We ate of the tree of the knowledge of good and evil. Now, we know what that means, as He promised we would.

Some will say "Okay, but if God knew that would happen and that people would end up suffering, then why did He go ahead and create the risk that ended up in a failure that is so much suffering?" That is a really tough question that bothered me intensely as well. But, I had to face the reality that He wanted a relationship with humans so much, to share love with us being free to love Him back, that He was willing to do it. Even if it meant things would go bad and there would be suffering and loss. Would you want to ask someone to marry you if they had no choice, but *had to* say yes? You made them do it through force or some other control? So, he was willing to give us that freedom in saying yes to Him, and to each other. To have love, he *had to make us free to "not love."*

I go back to the parenting analogy and ask myself, if I could see the future, like He can, and knew that my daughter would one day drink and drive, would I still teach her how to drive a car and have her have the freedom to make that choice? *Or more to the exact point, would I skip out on even having a daughter at all because she somehow somewhere will make a bad choice?* Well, apparently He still chose parenthood. He still wanted to afford his sons and daughters that freedom. Even knowing that it would all go bad. Ugh.

But there is more, and it makes it possible for everyone for it all to end well.

As much as He wanted freedom for us, and as much as He knew that we would misuse it, He had an option available to Him that we don't have. Knowing what He knew, He had an even bigger plan, where the pain and suffering would *not* win in the end after all. He loves us so much that He wasn't going to leave us and this world in the mess of our rejection of Him. Like any good, loving parent, He never gives up on His children, never abandons us, and searches for us to bring us back into connection and fix what we have broken. And the personal cost He had to pay to come rescue us and defeat evil and the suffering for good is incredible. God is not distant and unconcerned by suffering . . . but He does the unthinkable and unfathomable to do something about it. He became human. He died. He chose to suffer Himself to end our suffering. He chose to die to defeat our death.

He had a plan B that would end up with good winning over all of the evil in the end. He obviously knew we would fail, but in the very beginning, when we turned against Him, He revealed His next plan. His plan B had a name: Jesus. And it was the real plan A all along, when He knew we would use our freedom poorly.

He says in Genesis 3 that there would be a Savior, born of the seed of woman, meaning a human, who would be compelled by love to come rescue us, to crush the works of the tempter, and bring back all of those who want to come back to life. Eternally. And thereby would end all suffering. Right after the serpent engineers the Fall of mankind, God steps in and predicts how the movie will end, with good winning over evil:

> ***And I will put enmity between you [the tempter] and the woman, and between your seed and her seed.*** (Genesis 3:15 BSB)

God prophesied that He would send Jesus to later bring us home. To clear the path so we could come home and suffering would end. That meant doing something crazy. His paying the price of what we have broken. Taking the consequences of our rebellion onto Him. Like a parent paying a fine for a child's mistakes, so the cross is God paying for our mistakes. The cross also defeats death on our behalf. If unplugging from life results in death, then replugging into life is the end of death. That is why Jesus rose again; His resurrection was a natural consequence of defeating our sin. Death back to life.

In the crucifixion, though the cross is a profound thing to understand in its own right, Jesus reversed what we had broken. It says He was struck on the heel . . . "wounded," but not a final death blow. He was resurrected to life. But the tempter's work was crushed on the *head*. It was fatal. Death died the day of the resurrection of Jesus. One who was born of a woman, but not from the seed of man. The virgin birth was conceived by God and through a woman, *not* a man. That is why our "new birth" is a birth of the Spirit, and not just the earthly birth we have as fallen humans, from the seed that came from a human man. God predicted this redemption all along, from the beginning, to win in the end, in the perfect time to bring it about. The Savior "born of a woman."

> ***But when the set time had fully come, God sent his Son, born of a woman, born under the law, to redeem those under the law, that we might receive adoption to sonship.*** (Galatians 4:4)

God wins. He gets what He wanted all along: a love relationship with His humans who really want Him. Even when it all went bad He had a plan that would bring it all back to good, for all who want to come. For all who want Him. And we win too.

So, the big answer for me was (summarized) to understand that God is Love, and He wanted a love relationship with His children. To have that, He had to grant them freedom. He was willing to get that love relationship, even if it involved a "fall," or a big mistake along the path. Freedom required risk. I guess we could have not chosen to turn against God . . . to not sin. Yes, since there was free will. But we didn't. He knew it, though, I would assume, since He can see the future, and He already had a way to return us to freedom so love could reign forever. As Paul says, "It is for freedom that Christ has set us free" (Galatians 5:1). Freedom had to exist in the beginning, and it has to exist now. He even *still* gives people the freedom to reject Him, as some did and still do: "You are unwilling to come to Me so that you may have life" (John 5:40 AMP). He is plainly telling those who would not believe in Him and follow Him that they had the freedom to do so but were unwilling.

So, while we do live in a world with pain and suffering, for me, there is a good explanation as to why. God gave us freedom, and we chose against life. The result is a world that is experiencing death, daily and ongoing. And it is terrible, as He promised it would be if humans went against Him and left the relationship by trying to be our own god. It does not go well . . . the first chapters of this book pretty much show how that was true in my own life. But thankfully, getting reconnected saved my life. But even with that, and even with my accepting the reality of free will, another truth was and still is hard for me to accept as well: Why so long? Why does He let it go on?

THE "WHY HAS THOU FORSAKEN ME?" TIMES IN LIFE

Yes, God had a plan to make it all perfect again, if we want it. And yes, one day that will be totally complete. We get glimpses of His healing now, as He is present and brings life out of our death experiences. I have shared many of my experiences of His bringing me life in various ways in previous chapters. But the other truth that is hard to swallow is that He does not always do that. He is not doing it all fully right now. That is the second part of this objection of the "problem of pain," as C. S. Lewis called it. We do suffer, and there is unspeakable evil in the world. Even after Jesus came and was resurrected. I can understand that the freedom option is what caused it originally, but why does He allow it to continue? Why does He allow it to go on? Why is there suffering in this age between the fall of the earth and its final redemption? Why doesn't He just fix it all now?

The answer I found?

There is not one.

At least one that satisfies me or probably everyone, like we really want. Now, let me squirrel out on that for a minute. There are some partial answers to that, in my view. By "partial," I mean that they do not fully satisfy me, even though they help and explain some things. But I will share first why I do not think there is one, at least that we can understand.

In truth, if God is God and infinitely loving, infinitely good, infinitely powerful, and infinitely just, then there certainly *is* an answer. The answer is that He would do nothing evil or unjust or unloving. He *is* Love as the Bible says. He *is* fairness. He *is* compassion. So I am certain that He knows all the answers of why He has allowed this season of suffering to go on until Jesus comes back and makes it all new again. With heaven and the new earth, which will be perfect, as He has promised, suffering will one day end. But why the "wait till then" approach? I am sure that He knows why He is doing it this way, and it all makes sense . . . just not to me.

And here is why having no full answer to that is something that I can stomach and hate at the same time: Again, it is because the Bible says that there is no answer He will give us, other than the one I have to accept: "Trust Me." That is the only real answer that He gives other than He is going to make it all right in the end and He knows what He is doing. He says in many places, "I am not going to explain everything now. You have to trust Me."

There are several examples of God answering that question that way in the Scriptures, but none better than Job and Jesus.

I don't know how much you know about the story of Job, but it pretty much is the story of what we have been talking about: Why does God allow humanity to go through this? Why do bad things happen to good people? Part of that we have seen is because of our freedom misused. But that is just how humanity got into the mess in the beginning. It does not answer "Why doesn't He just fix it now? Why does He allow it to go on?" Job gives us the real answer from God, which is basically that there is no answer. "I am God, trust Me" was His only answer to Job.

Job was a good man. "Blameless" is the word the Bible uses. When we ask "Why do bad things happen to good and innocent people?" we are talking about Job. And for some reason, God allowed him to go through horrendous suffering. He lost his physical health, all of his possessions, the well-earned respect of others, and way worst of all, his children. His suffering was extreme, as the Bible is very clear about. So bad, he cried, "Why did I not perish at birth; why did I not die as I came from the womb?" (Job 3:11 BSB), a point similar to "Why have children to begin with?" It was so bad, his wife even said to him, "Do you still retain your integrity? Curse God and die!" (Job 2:9 BSB).

He endured it, but while he was in it, he longed to die, as he longed to have never been born. He was innocently suffering and longing to die, as I have heard the same longing for death from many patients who were enduring the suffering that came from abuse that they did not cause. And as has happened to many of you, to add insult to injury, the people around him hurt him even more in his suffering. His friends blamed him for his suffering when, in fact, he did nothing to cause it. Satan was the one attempting to get him to turn away from God, something he has always done with all humans since the Creation. Sometimes he does it through inflicting suffering on people, as well as sometimes using pleasure and other temptations to lure them to destruction (Adam and Eve). But his friends said he was suffering because of his own sin and lack of faith and other shortcomings, the essence of "victim blaming." A lie.

As they tried to give answers, Job protested it all in pain, telling them their answers were worthless, and he wished they would just shut up. But Job never turned away from God. He raged, he argued his case, and he expressed all of the universal human emotions that innocent suffering brings out in us when we are assaulted by destructive forces in life and can do nothing about it. All the while, God, for some reason that we cannot understand and certainly Job couldn't, was allowing this to go on for a while. That is what Job, like us, could never understand. And he protested it and argued about it. It was just not fair. But, before the argument ended, Job did have one thing carrying him through: he still trusted that God was good. He never gave up on God's goodness. He held out hope, because he knew that God was good.

> ***Though He slay me, I will hope in Him.*** (Job 13:15 BSB)

Job's answer to the question at first was that, even though he could not understand it and gave all the arguments he could come up with and all of the expressed emotions, he was just going to trust Him. Then, after all that he had argued with God, he finally gets God's answer to all of the questions about why we suffer.

God's answer was simple and, as I said, a "non-answer" for what we want. Paraphrased, His message to Job was "My wisdom and understanding of your suffering is so much higher than yours that you will never be able to understand it. But I am God, and you are not." Here are a few excerpts:

> ***Who is this who obscures My counsel by words without knowledge? Now brace yourself like a man; I will question you, and you shall inform Me. Where were you when I laid the foundations of the earth? Tell Me, if you have understanding. Who fixed its measurements? Surely you know! Or who stretched a measuring line across it? On what were its***

> ***foundations set, or who laid its cornerstone, while the morning stars sang together and all the sons of God shouted for joy?*** (Job 38:2–7 BSB)

God continues to list a zillion things He has done to prove to us how infinite His wisdom and goodness is, such as creating the heavens, the seas, the animals, and many, many very complicated aspects of creation that we read about earlier, and others.

He lists all of them, and says, "If you are so smart to question my justice and goodness, where were you when I did all of that?" Said another way, "I know a wee bit more about what wisdom, goodness, justice, and fairness is than you do. Who are you to question me?" And if you read it, it is not a short few sentences from God to Job about who knows more. It is a lot of material that God comes out with about how much higher He is than Job. He does not give the answer we want, but He convinces Job that He is Someone who knows the answer. And that is enough for Job.

After seeing God and hearing his response, Job finally says:

> ***I know that you can do anything, and no one can stop you. You asked, "Who is this that questions my wisdom with such ignorance?" It is I—and I was talking about things I knew nothing about, things far too wonderful for me. You said, "Listen and I will speak! I have some questions for you, and you must answer them." I had only heard about you before, but now I have seen you with my own eyes. I take back everything I said, and I sit in dust and ashes to show my repentance."*** (Job 42:2–6 NLT)

Basically, the answer from God is "I am not going to answer your questioning me about My goodness and fairness. I am just going to remind you of Who I am, and if you really get it, you will be humbled forever even questioning my fairness. I do know more than you. Period. Remember Who I am, and trust Me." That is all we get.

That is what I mean when I said "there is no answer." Specifically, God never answers the "why" question. He gives us a "Who" answer. It comes down to the one basic theme of the whole Bible: faith in God. "Who" he is. "Trust Me." Even when you do not understand. And when Job saw Him and heard Him, it was enough for him, the one who had suffered.

And while that is "no answer" to the "why" that we all want to know, it is an answer: "It is too high for you to understand." And I struggled with that, because I felt like it was not enough. My emotions in and about suffering were the same as Jesus' when He suffered on the cross. I mentioned earlier that we see the answer in the stories of both Job and Jesus: "there is no answer" other than to have faith that God knows what He is doing. When Jesus was on the cross, he said it this way:

> ***And at three in the afternoon Jesus cried out in a loud voice, "Eloi, Eloi, lema sabachthani?" (which means "My God, my God, why have you forsaken me?").*** (Mark 15:34)

Jesus, in his humanity, felt the same way. He could not understand why His Father seemingly had forsaken Him. But of course, as we well know, God did. God understood why. And behind it all, God *was* still all loving, all powerful, and all good. Even when we cannot understand it. And that same cry is throughout the psalms and other stories the Bible gives us when people suffer. We do not understand the "why," and yet God does, and He is still good. We can trust Him even when we do not understand Him. Jesus did not understand it at that moment as a tortured man, but there was an answer higher than anyone's ways, and the answer was one of God's ultimate goodness: His love for mankind. And remember, He was *also* God. He *chose* to suffer and die for us. This was not some cosmic "child abuse," as some have tried to claim. He came on purpose, to take our place in death, and end it forever.

Personally, I did not have the ability to emotionally accept this truth very well until my training as a psychologist, when I learned about how our cognitive understanding works. When studying Piaget, who, in addition to being the heralded psychologist who first postulated how our intellect develops, was also an epistemologist (that is the science of "how do we know we know?"). An important concept he taught was that a child literally cannot understand certain things until she gets to a higher level of ability to understand. Her mind just cannot wrap itself around something too high for it to make add up and work.

A simple example is something called object permanence. A very young child does not know that an object still exists when they can no longer see it. You cannot play hide and seek with a child who has not achieved object permanence. If you hide a ball, they lose interest. Out of sight, out of mind. There is no longer a ball. So why seek it?

But they get to a higher level of cognitive ability to understand. They get to a point where they realize that the ball still exists even when they can't see it. So, they will look for it. They will search for the ball that exists but is hiding somewhere. Before that, there were realities that they could not understand, even when those realities were true and very clear to an adult. Just like a parent can understand the ball still exists and a child can't, God can understand suffering when we can't. If you have a problem with Piaget's theory, then just think about trying to teach algebra to a five-year-old. One day they will get it, but not that day. They just can't understand it. Some understanding takes a higher cognitive ability than we may possess at the time.

A very young child gets taken to the doctor and gets a painful shot. She screams at her parent: "How can you let this happen to me? If you love me, how can you let this happen?" is what she must be feeling if she could put it all into words. "Where are you?"

All the while, the parent does understand the "why" and knows that he or she loves that child as much as is possible. They know that the suffering is *not* because they do not love their little one. And it breaks their heart to see the pain. But, they have something good in mind in the end. They get it, even when the child does not.

For the child, they just are incapable of "getting it." Literally incapable, yet it is still true. *Now, this in no way means that God is causing or allowing horrible things happen to you for a personal reason in your life.* People often, not God, have chosen to do things that have caused you to suffer. God didn't do that. Or, the diseased creation, the "fallen" creation with its death cancer living in it, brought it into your life. God is not behind evil. He hates our suffering. It is why I often struggle with the phrase people use with someone who is suffering greatly: "Well, you know, everything happens for a reason." *Yes, but the reason is that we live in a fallen world. God didn't cause it.*

What I am referring to here with the child analogy is simply that when I can't understand why He sometimes allows horrible things to happen, and does not prevent them, or waits seemingly *forever* to do something about it, I can accept that I do not understand nor do I have an answer for that. I can accept that I have limited understanding. But, like the child cannot understand, I still can't understand why He isn't calling an end to evil and suffering yet. I really can't. But I do believe He has reasons for waiting to end all suffering that I am just not big enough to comprehend. When I really understood this concept: *there are things that can be true, and seem wrong to me, but I just cannot understand them*, my doubts began to go back to sleep, or at least take a rest. I learned a different level of trust and faith in God, knowing that he was good even when it does not look like he is even paying attention. It may defy all of my logical reasoning. But, God has a higher level of understanding than I do. He knows some things (ha!) that I don't. His ways are above my ways, as the Bible says, and His thoughts are above my thoughts (Isaiah 55:9). He has a level of understanding that I cannot and will ever be able to approach. He knows why He is waiting, even when I don't. I still don't get it.

I don't know if that helps you, but it changed everything for me.

It is still not the answer I want. But I am not as smart or as loving or as just or as wise as God. And because of how much bigger He is than I am, I will, like Job, surrender my judgment of His infinite fairness. I will accept that He knows something I do not, even when it seems to make no sense. And I know that He is both good and all powerful. I will trust Him. And I will tell Him how terrible it is for me at the same time.

As I said, the free-will argument suffices for me, even though there are questions that it raises that I am not smart enough to understand. You might have some of those even as you read the above. It is still mysterious. But, for me, it came down to having to trust that He knows it all. And why would I trust that? *That is why Jesus is so important.* He came to not only die for us but also to show us what God is actually like. Jesus said to Philip, "Anyone who has seen Me has seen the Father" (John 14:9). We can know what God is like through seeing Jesus.

Compassionate, not sadistic or uncaring. Or asleep at the wheel. Caring about suffering enough to suffer and die to end ours. While I have unanswered questions, I look at Him, seeing what He was like, and I can rest with my unanswered questions. "A very good God has got this" is all I know in the depths of my soul.

Now, in another direction of pain and suffering, I do understand a little more about *some* aspects of suffering at this point in my journey, and also how *some* ways we suffer can be good (not the aspects of innocent people who suffer from abuse, or evil inflicted upon them, or illnesses that are because of the diseased universe as I mentioned above. That is just a horrible result of this world gone bad. God never wants that. It is the devil that Jesus said comes to steal and destroy in John 10:10).

What I am referring to is that I can now understand how the specific kinds of suffering that are in the service of growth can be a good thing. After decades of practicing as a psychologist, I have often intentionally led people into deeper levels of pain in order for them to be healed, for example. I can readily say "some pain is good for us." Facing painful feelings is curative when done well. Or pushing a person into very scary aspects of fear or anxiety in order to cure it. Or seeing them go through some struggles that I know are going to make them better in the end, like doing an intervention on an addict. I have admitted many people to hospitals as they screamed at me to let them go. I can feel for them in the process, but I do not hesitate at all in leading them into it, nor do I feel bad about it . . . even though I feel empathy for how hard it is for them, I know they will get better as a result, even though it sucks to be admitting to a hospital against one's will! But I am leading them into suffering that can heal them. I get that. I will always choose to help someone enter suffering when I know it is going to help them. If I know it is for their best. "Kids, go do your homework." Even they sometimes see *that* as unbearable pain . . . but it will help them get a job one day.

So, some suffering we endure for good reasons, and I can also even see what the Bible means when it says that God can bring good out of even some of the worst things that happen to us. Things that He did *not cause or lead us into.* He did not cause the suffering in those cases, and it is not the person's fault (e.g., Job), but He can still use it for good in our lives. When He did not heal my hand in college and I lost my ability to play competitive golf, I could not understand it. I prayed, and nothing happened. But He was able to use that loss for my good and bring a greater healing. At the same time, I am sure that He felt compassion for what I was going through. He entered it and helped me heal.

But still . . . it is fraught with mystery. I still cannot understand when innocent people are hurt or suffer and there is no good in it at all. One thing that does help me, though . . . He can bring some good out of it. Not because of it, like there was some divine purpose for it, but entering into it and doing some amazingly restorative things, and He will join them in it and bring some relief, and He often brings good things to the sufferer, and He does. But that kind of suffering itself is not good in itself in any measure. It is the Universe Gone Bad. It is the death sentence. Cancer is not good. But God can enter into that scenario and show His love and work in it to bring something good out of something so bad. Even when He does not heal it, for whatever unknown reason I just still do not get.

We do know, though, that God hurts when we suffer. He says that it grieves Him when people suffer because of the abuse of others, the evil and selfishness of others, or other horrible realities. He empathizes with the sufferer and is relieved Himself when we enter in and relieve people's suffering. For example, when we give to the hungry or help the infirmed. He says that when you help a suffering person, "you did it unto Me!" (see Matthew 25:40). He is suffering *with* the hungry, the thirsty, the sick, the poor, the imprisoned. But when you help them, and their suffering is lessened, *He feels His suffering for them gets relieved.* He feels their pain so much that when you help them, it relieves the pain that He feels! That shows that He cares when we suffer. He is with us. *He does not like it that it is happening to us or them. He hates it. He died to end it.*

There is no good answer to "why" other than the misused freedom given to man that turned evil, and now man also inflicts that evil upon others. But remember, the Bible talks about an evil personal devil, Satan, who has an entire army who daily tempts people to do destructive things, and causes a lot of suffering on the earth. And like the Genesis story says, we sometimes open ourselves up in some way to be used in his plot against God. We sometimes desire activities (think drugs or sexual addiction) or devise plans that are not good for us. Or we side with our dark sides and unwittingly become instruments of evil. You probably have known people who choose to fuel their anger and it turns into destructive hatred and gets acted out on others. Mankind often offers themselves to be used by Satan to do evil and inflict suffering without knowing they are being used, as the enemy of God carries out his long-term war. Ultimately he will lose when God wraps up the bigger story of this universe which is in a war of good versus evil. That is coming.

The message of the Bible is clear: God hates suffering and evil so much that one day He will avenge it all and make it right. He promises that in the end, it will all be made right. He will pour out His judgment on those who do evil to others and who never repent or make it right. And Satan will be defeated. And through that process, He has invited all of us to join Him in that ultimate victory.

So, the answer to suffering that some people give when a child dies, "God works in mysterious ways," falls short. While God is in ultimate control . . . He is not the author of that suffering, and

He certainly does not like it. On the contrary, He feels deeply for it and wants us to partner with Him to end it.

So, I do not know why He can allow it to go on, even for another minute. But there is some reason, which we cannot understand, why He can allow something that He hates, the suffering of humans, to continue for a while. But for some reason, He does allow it. And He will end it one day.

So for now, many times in the midst of the suffering, we can only agree with Piaget's principle: "I cannot understand how there can be a ball that exists when I cannot see it." And with Job, "I cannot understand why all of this is happening to me, or to someone else, but I will trust Him." And we can know that He is not the author of this suffering, as Jesus told us this very specifically. He said the devil is the one who "comes only to steal and kill and destroy; I have come that they may have life, and have it to the full" (John 10:10). He said that if you have seen Jesus, you have seen the Father, God.

And we know for sure that Jesus was all about relieving suffering and stopping injustice. He did it every single day He was on earth. Jesus did not cause suffering, but He came to end it. And if you have seen Him, you have seen God.

One last good thing I will add about how suffering can be used for good that shows the compassion and goodness of God. *He can use our suffering to help others.* How many times have you been helped by someone, possibly a friend or therapist, who is able to help you like no one else can, because they themself have been through what you are suffering with? The "wounded healer" is a reality. They truly know how you feel, to the extent that is possible. I know that going through my depression and God showing me the way out has made me a much better psychologist than I would have been had I never been through it and had He never shown me compassion to heal me. If you know anyone who has gotten sober through a twelve-step program, you'll know that all of the help throughout the program comes from those whom God helped, and now they share His compassion to the next person. That is the twelfth step of the program. As is written in Romans 8, God is able to use all things we go through in some good way, so that even the worst suffering might be a benefit to someone, and sometimes even us. He didn't cause it for our good, but He is able to use it for good in some way. This is one of my favorite verses that speaks to that:

> ***Praise be to the God and Father of our Lord Jesus Christ, the Father of compassion and the God of all comfort, who comforts us in all our troubles, so that we can comfort those in any trouble with the comfort we ourselves receive from God.*** (2 Corinthians 1:3–4)

So, I began with saying this one was the toughest one for me. And I hope you have seen that I do not even know and understand all of the "why." I am left with more questions and answers. But, somewhat like Job, I can say that I do know that He is good. I can trust that even when I don't understand why I can't see the reason for His not making it better . . . the worst "ball behind the couch." But, I know my Father knows what is going on, and what I have seen and understood helps me with what I can't see or understand. What I have experienced myself and know from others' lives, and seeing who Jesus was in the Gospels, convinces me that He is a God of love, who hates evil and suffering.

It is a great mystery still, but I am okay now with waiting to know the final answer one day when I see Him. I do believe "He's got this."

Twelve

Psychology and Faith

I have been in the field of psychology for many decades now. Including being a student, decades of clinical practice, conducting research, being clinical director for an entire system of hospital units and treatment centers, and decades of performance and leadership consulting. Add to that continuing education throughout that time to stay current with the latest research and findings in psychology and neuroscience. It has been a long journey, and it is interesting to look back at that path and see how psychology proved the Bible to be true for me. And the proving grounds did not begin with the science. Actually, surprisingly, it was the Bible that had to rescue me from the "psychology" that I was learning from the church. My first few years of faith, as a psychology graduate student and "churchgoer" and reader of many Christian "psychology" books, I learned all of the models of how the two go together. I did not know enough at that time to see their deficiencies. So I accepted what they were saying. Many in the faith world saw secular psychology as being antithetical to faith, coming from a humanistic worldview having little to offer. Others integrated it somewhat, picking and choosing what they liked.

There were models that taught that clinical issues all came from sins that were in need of repentance, or not knowing enough Bible to have in your heads to order your thinking to wellness, spiritual, or supernatural experiences of emotional healing, or deliverance from demons and spiritual oppression, for example.

Certainly, there is some truth in all of those arenas. Our own "sins" can cause a lot of suffering . . . think of wrecked homes, for example, from bad behavior, or lives destroyed through addiction and character disorders. Of course, self-destructive thinking can cause a lot of pain, as the science in cognitive therapy has proven. And for sure, the need for God to touch our broken hearts and trauma is real, and He does; there are countless testimonies of that reality, including my own. You can wonder about the existence of the supernatural and other spiritual areas if you are a materialist, but many psychologists will attest to some "wicked" stuff they have seen that they cannot explain, which certainly at least seems supernatural at the time.

But as much as I saw some truth in all of those models, as I gained more and more clinical experience, the Christian models began to fall short of both my scientific understanding of the bigger picture, as well as my clinical experience. And here was the experience that threw me into a mini crisis of faith: what I was learning to be true clinically, and scientifically, was not what many of the "Christian" models proposed.

Mostly because I saw them fall short . . . people were not getting well a lot of times when they had had much treatment in those models of the "Christian way" of treating mental health issues. And all of those were touted as the "biblical" way, even though much within those models disagreed with each other. I chuckle at how many people call their system of change to be "God's" way, while disagreeing with the other "God's" way. Makes God look confused as to what His way is, it seems to me.

And, past that . . . here is what really threw me: I was learning that there were real clinical modalities and interventions and approaches to therapy that worked. I was seeing eating disorders healed, depression healed, anxiety states overcome, thought disorders "cured," trauma healed, and the like. I was falling in love with my field as I saw the fruits of clinical practice. I loved my clinical work.

But in falling in love with all of that, I felt like I was an adulterer . . . my new love seemingly was not the love I was supposed to have with my faith and the Bible. It was a spiritual crisis almost as severe as my first one of "Where is God?" I saw people getting well . . . but where was the faith as I understood it in all of this? I was beginning to feel like two people: one who believed in my Christian faith, and one who believed in the truth that I was seeing before me that seemed to be in conflict with my Christian faith. Did I have to be a "science denier"? It felt like it. I still was using prayer and the Bible and *knew* that helped, but not in the ways that some of the systems of "Christian" counseling was espousing.

So, I decided to resolve this dilemma no matter what it took. I *knew* God was real. And I *knew* that the Bible was true in the ways we have discussed previously. But many of the Christian views I had learned of psychology were just not completely true, or, at the very least, where there was truth, fell short. I knew too much to go back to thinking they were right or accepting them as they were being presented. I could not live with that, so here is what I did. I basically dropped out of life for the better part of a couple of years.

Of course, I still worked and played golf . . . couldn't stop those. ☺ But every other waking moment I decided to do one thing: just read and study my Bible. I was not going to read any of the Christian stuff about psychology or mental health issues and what they had to say. I already knew that literature. I wanted to see what the

Bible itself said about these issues. Just on its own, as I looked at it through the lenses of my clinical and scientific expertise that I had gained over those years. And here is what happened:

I was "born again again."

I could not believe it. Literally everything I was learning in the science that showed where mental health, relational, and performance issues came from, as well as how to resolve them, was right there in the Scriptures. All along, it was all there.

The causes and cures of those issues were throughout the Bible, and much of the "Christian" material that one reads was *not* there and, not only that, was actually even taught against! It was much like my previous chapter on bad-behaving Christians. People reject the Bible because they see the falsehood of some Christians and think that is what the faith is about, but as I have shown, the Bible sometimes agrees with the skeptics, not the other way around. In this case, the Bible supported my skepticism of the things some of the church was teaching and, instead, was agreeing with the science of psychology! (I am sure I will get some angry emails from some for that proposition, but that's not new. I have had those debates for decades. Feel free to send them.) Remember, when Job suffered, God chastened the religious counselors for not speaking the truth, too. Religious people don't always get it right. They gave Job all of the "Christian" answers of the time, and they were wrong too.

So, after a period of deep study, my conflict was resolved. But more than resolved . . . I had a new life mission in a sense. I could now really help people get unconflicted, but more than that, I could show them and others that the Bible really does know why you suffer and that what God says there can help you. So, I ended up writing a lot of books on that topic, and I still do.

And it has been an amazing journey, for which I am grateful to God. One capstone I think back on that was particularly fulfilling was that after John and I designed treatment centers and hospital units that used all these faith- and science-based clinical treatment methods, we opened them up to outside university researchers. After their clinical research, that treatment program was documented to get better results than others that were non-faith-based in treating Axis 1 (DSM) clinical issues and, surprisingly for many, Axis 2 issues (personality disorders) as well. This research was presented at the American Psychological Association's annual meeting and was surprisingly well received. It was a real highlight of all of this work.

My books *Changes That Heal*, *Boundaries*, and *How People Grow* (by myself and John Townsend) came out of this work and this season.

And all along the way, I have had a blast. It is surprising to me as well as how many people just do not know what the Bible has to offer in these areas that psychology addresses. I fondly recall a conversation I had with a woman on an airplane one day.

"So what do you do?" she asked.

Usually, on airplanes, I do not answer this question, as I know what is going to come. The person often wants to tell me about some problem, and I am in for a four-hour session when I was hoping to binge a Netflix series. But for some reason, that day, I let it slip.

"I am a psychologist," I said.

"Oh my gosh," she said. "I have to tell you about my boyfriend."

(Here we go . . .) I sighed.

"So, what's the issue?" I asked.

"I just broke up with him again . . . and I am heartbroken. I can't believe we are in this situation again, but I just couldn't do it anymore." She began to cry. "We break up because I can't live with it, and then I miss him so much. He comes back to me, and then I take him back because I love him, and it is good for a minute, and then it all happens again, and I can't take it and I break up. But then I miss him and we get back together again. And now it has happened again," she explained.

"What happens again that is so painful you can't live with?" I queried.

"His anger," she said. "He just gets so angry, and it is so hurtful, and I also get kind of scared."

"What is he angry about?" I asked.

"Whenever I don't do what he wants, he gets angry. He tries to control me and if I don't want to, he rages." She went on. "He won't listen to what hurts me."

"So, what do you do then?" I wondered aloud. "What makes it better?"

"Well, I know how to calm him down. I just do whatever he wants, and then he is fine. We have peace . . . but I can't always do that. I sometimes just *can't*, but then he gets enraged, and then I do whatever he wants and things are good again. But I just can't live like that." She cried. "I can calm him down by agreeing with him, but I can't always just give in. I feel like I am not a person and am losing myself. So, we break up and then I go back."

"Well," I said. "There is an old saying: 'If you rescue an angry man, you will only have to do it again.' Keep going back and rescuing him from his anger by complying, and you will calm him down, but it will only repeat itself."

"Wait . . . what was that saying again?" she asked.

"If you rescue an angry man, you will only have to do it again," I repeated.

"That is *amazing*!" she exclaimed. "Where did you get that?"

"The Bible," I said.

"Wait . . ." she said. "*That's* in the Bible?"

"Yep. Proverbs 19:19. Go check it out," I told her. "You should read it sometime. There is good stuff in there."

"I never knew that was in the *Bible*!" she said.

"Yeah, I know. I didn't either, until I started to really read it."

We talked some more, and I told her a little about my story. But what had stood out for me throughout my journey was that there are a zillion ways psychology validates the Scriptures. The terms "rescuer" or "enabler" became popular in addiction science in the last century, but the Bible had said for centuries that rescuing someone with a character problem would never work. (Try just being nicer to a malignant narcissist, and see where it gets you. There are many verses advising against that.) The Bible usually prescribes limits and boundaries, which sometimes will help and will protect you from them. Addictionologists began to discover codependency in the middle of the last century, which says that the addict is not the only one who has a problem—the one who was enabling them by letting them off the hook and not confronting it with boundaries was part of the overall problem as well. Awesome discovery by science, right?

Not exactly. Awesome validation of what Moses has said when he was giving us God's ways so we might always thrive, as I discussed earlier. He said that when we fail to set limits and confront someone because they are either weak/needy or powerful (the two reasons we usually don't set limits on bad behavior . . . either we overidentify with their weakness or neediness and do not require them to do what is needed for them to get well, or we are afraid to confront them, as in my seatmate's case, because of their "power"), just as the addictionologists and nowadays the "how to deal with narcissists" gurus will tell you correctly, we keep the problem going. They are usually not going to change by your giving in to them. That is what she was doing with her boyfriend. Only limits might help (see Leviticus 19:15,17). (Sometimes, though someone may need help with those limits, as in some cases, the angry one is also dangerous. Seek help if that is you, and do not put yourself in a dangerous scenario with an abusive person.)

Anyway, I found that she was like me and a lot of others. Oftentimes, we just do not know what the Bible says about these issues. I had been in the church at this point for several years, yet I had never been taught about "boundaries" in the church. I learned that from the science of psychology. And then, when I went back to the Bible, there it was all along, in a million passages. I was amazed at how many Christians had never known that the Bible taught that you should set limits with people, and not only just "love" them or be "forgiving." While forgiveness and love are true, many had seen only those sides of the Bible's teachings, not the limits that the Bible also supports.

That is just one little example of a tip from a much bigger metapsychology that the Scriptures actually teach. And that is what got me interested and began to further validate my faith, another pillar of "why I believe."

Most of the etiologies (causes) of mental health issues fall into a small group of issues. In other words, most mental health problems that are not biologically rooted come from a handful of human issues that manifest themselves in various clinical, relational, and performance symptoms. (Said another way, many of the same symptoms can come from the same underlying issue.) These human issues are basically what the Bible is about. It names them over and over and, beyond that, gives us the processes that cure them. I have never seen an evidence-based treatment, one that has been proven to work, in which the underlying process involved is not an issue the Bible covers. That is what blew my mind, and it still does. Here are just some that validate it for me.

1. The issue of attachment, bonding, and connection versus human emotional isolation, disruptive connection, or lack of connection

This is the primary, number one problem the Bible says caused everything else. We were designed for connection to God and to others from the beginning. When we broke connection with Him, we lost our source of life, which is unbroken relationship. Both with God, but also with other humans. Said simply, broken relationship is the problem, and restoring connection is the answer to that problem.

The psychology of human development, clinical psychology, and performance psychology have borne this out. Developmental delays, brain development, physical development, immune systems as well as most everything else can be affected by the absence of or complications and injuries in the attachment process. Beyond developmental delays, psychological illnesses are myriad that can be connected to attachment issues, from clinical problems like depression, anxiety, and addictions, to relational dysfunction as well. Emotional isolation of the heart and disconnectedness is a major cause of many mental health problems. The list of symptoms is endless.

In the Bible as well as in psychology, the process for healing connection issues is explained in exactly the same way: a safe "love object" to attach to; overcoming the need-fear dilemma through vulnerable expressions of need and pain, to finding emotional attunement, empathy, love, and understanding from a "safe person" on the other end. The Bible and psychology both give exactly the same tasks, responses, and process involved in healing this "basic fault," as the great psychologist Michael Balint termed it. Genesis would say it is the "basic fault" as well, and the rest of the Bible affirms it and calls us to healing one another through empathy, kindness, support, containment, responsiveness, compassion, and many other directives. The result, as the New Testament says, is having hearts "knit together by strong ties of love" (Colossians 2:2 NLT). When a therapy group fosters connectedness and heals the fear, defenses, or resistance to connection, they are using proven therapeutic processes and agreeing with the Bible about the problem and its resolution.

Every deep system of therapy that is proven begins with something called the therapeutic alliance, where safety and connection can make way for the healing process that will follow, and that same connection will drive the internalization of love and structure from the outside that will become psychological emotional regulatory systems within the person. Said another way, a lack of good relationship injures us, and good ones heal us.

2. The issue of freedom, separateness, autonomy, boundaries, differentiation, and control

As psychology teaches, once a person learns to be connected in a relationship (from primary caregivers through the rest of life), the next issue that has to be mastered is freedom from our love object. In other words, when one loves someone and is loved by that person, although remaining in the connection in a deep way, they must be free from that person and free from their control: mental, emotional, and physical. This issue of personal autonomy and the ability to make choices for oneself is called agency. It follows that when we have agency, we have self-control and a host of other psychological abilities. When we do not feel that sense of personal agency, we suffer. Clinical issues again such as depression, anxiety states, panic attacks, eating disorders, some OCD, addictions, and others can often be related to a person's inability to establish autonomy from the ones they love and have self-directed control of themself. Said another way: boundaries.

Codependency, and the depression and anxiety that come from this fusion and crossover of boundaries and responsibility, follow.

Being able to separate from one's family, to "leave and cleave" and become one's own person, is related to this issue as well, a whole arena of psychology that family systems theory and family therapy emphasize. Virtually all therapeutic systems offer something for this issue in some way, from AA's Serenity Prayer to assertiveness training in behavioral therapy, and many others. One's inability to establish personal agency and regain free choice runs throughout the interventions of all sorts of therapies and is documented to be efficacious throughout the literature.

The Bible teaches that "It is for freedom that Christ has set us free" (Galatians 5:1). And it would be impossible to list all of the teachings of the Bible along the line of being free from others' control, and establishing boundaries and limits to contain the destructiveness of other people upon oneself (see Matthew 18:15–19, for example).

Boundaries and limits on destructive behavior are taught throughout the Bible, and regaining control for oneself is a chief tenet. In the Scriptures, this ability is called self-control (see Galatians 5:23). The Bible rails against the oppression of anyone and always is a champion for helping others regain their freedom. Self-control is heralded, and control of others is condemned.

Clinical, relational, and performance issues always involve a growth and regaining of one's freedom, self-definition, autonomy, agency, and the like. Can you even imagine a world where people would always have self-control, able to control/regulate their own emotions, impulses, and behavior; and be able to be separate from the control and dysfunction of others? That is a goal that the Bible and all of psychology emphasize wholeheartedly. Past the alignment of the principle of freedom being important, I also saw that all of the therapeutic interventions aimed at helping people regain this freedom and self-control were exactly the same ones that the Scriptures prescribed. I had rarely heard these preached from the pulpit, but when I went back to the Bible they were all there.

3. The conflict between the coexistence of "good" and "bad"

The fact that we were designed to be perfect people in a perfect world and lost it results in our being ill-equipped to deal with the existence of pain, loss, trauma, failure, grief, and other experiences. We know what life ought to be like, and yet we find it otherwise, and we are not harnessed to metabolize that coexistence.

Much of psychology centers around this problem of pain, as we have called it earlier, but more by focusing on its pure existence in our lives and how to metabolize it and deal with it well. Said simply, it is not supposed to be there. So, our systems do not know how to deal with it, how to process all of the pain, failure, woundedness, and disappointment that we feel. Much of psychology focuses on how to deal with that pain and help people develop the needed abilities and skills. We do not come into the world able to handle it, and past that, our abilities to handle it are often further broken themselves, through trauma or other destructive events we encounter. We have this pain, and our equipment to process it fails us. Beyond that, we are separated from the connections that would help us build those skills as well, as I said above.

Developmental psychology shows us that early on, as I mentioned in an earlier chapter, we can't put good and bad together. We split them. We love someone when they make us happy, and hate them when they frustrate us. Have you ever known someone who thought you were wonderful until you disappointed them in some way, and then you became, in their eyes, the worst person ever? That can even happen in a moment with some personality disorders, such as borderline personality disorder or narcissism. You instantly go from "all good" to "all bad" in their eyes, over even the smallest infraction. The relational disturbances that come from this are, obviously, myriad. Most people do not walk to the altar at their wedding feeling like they do the day they decide to divorce. "All good" turned to "all bad."

But way past the more severe forms of splitting, as psychology shows, we all struggle with metabolizing living in an imperfect world. Clinical issues such as depression, anxiety states, addictions, and eating disorders can all be related to not being able to live with the imperfections of ourselves and others, and the wounds and losses inflicted upon us. In fact, one of the most popular therapies of our day, cognitive behavioral therapy, is almost totally dedicated to changing the thinking patterns of how people appraise the "negative" in life, trying to help them think about failure or imperfection or negative events in a more regulated, balanced, and integrated way. Dialectical behavior therapy works on the aspects of splitting as well, as does all of psychodynamic therapy. Freud and Breuer showed over a century ago that the repression of negative emotional experiences that could not be metabolized was at the heart of several emotional problems, as well as Freud's further findings on the critical superego and its dynamics that cognitive therapy now addresses. If you have ever been told "you need to process your grief, face the pain, anger, and loss," you have received advice related to those early findings. And that is exactly what the Bible says over and over. I was surprised to find all of these effective methods of treatment in the Bible.

Therapies related to grief, trauma, overcoming failure, perfectionism, and many others are oriented toward dealing with this same issue: helping the ill-equipped human organism to gain the broken and lacking equipment needed to process the problem of pain and the "bad stuff" in our existence.

The Bible affirms all of this. It speaks over and over about the resolution of grief and mourning, self-critical voices we carry inside (related to Freud's "superego" at times), criticism and judgment of others and ourselves, the need for forgiveness and reconciliation of broken relationships, and all of the other tools needed. Many, many clear directives given in the Bible teach the very same interventions that psychology does for how these emotional, cognitive, and relational dynamics are resolved.

One of my favorite moments in Scripture is when Solomon says in Ecclesiastes that it is better to process pain than to seek pleasure to avoid it, because as he said, a sad face can make a heart happy (see Ecclesiastes 7:3). Cry it out, and you will be better. Imagine that . . . thousands of years before Freud showed that getting in touch with pain instead of avoiding it can resolve "complicated bereavement," hysteria, and other maladies, the Bible had said it. Turns out, the Bible was there before science, but once again, science proved it to be true. Ask the lady on the airplane. ☺

4. The leveling of power that evolves from childhood to adulthood

Both the Bible and psychology affirm that a child comes into the world in a psychologically one-down position to the "big people." The parent has authority over the child's life. There is a power imbalance, for good reason. The big people know where the food is, and how to get the car to the playground. They set and enforce the rules using their authority, as do teachers and other authority figures. The child looks up to them, appropriately fears (respects in a good way) and respects their authority, and learns to obey them.

At the same time, they are internalizing skills and abilities from those big people and learning how to use them. These capacities are built and developed over the years. One day, after a slow, natural overthrow of the family government we call adolescence, the child's brain and body and skills and maturity get to the point where it is time to call it quits. They are no longer a child in an adult's world, but now they are "one of them." They can call their own shots and be the governing body of their own lives, with all of the privileges afforded therein. The Bible affirms this when it says that when we were children, "we were under guardians and managers until the date set by the father" (Galatians 4:2 NASB).

But, as psychology has shown us, we don't all get there unscathed. We get hurt and damaged by authority and can get stunted, or we internalize harsh authority voices into our heads, or we get so enraged by abusive authority that we develop an almost "necessary rebellion" to even survive. These are the results of negative parenting and are significantly damaging, leading to all sorts of emotional, clinical, relational, and performance problems. The "internalized parent" is often not a good one, and the internal relationship the person develops with their "parent inside" is not working. The "inner child" is still suffering inside the head as they continue to live with those parental failures, as psychology sometimes puts it. Or those internalizations and modeling are acted out onto others in abusive and toxic relationships, putting others in the one-down position to try to compensate for what they feel deep inside.

But harsh and hurtful parenting is not the only problem. There is also the parenting that did not happen . . . people were neglected as children or not supplied with the help to become mature grown-ups, and as a result they enter the adult world ill-equipped. The maturity needed to work with authority is lacking, and the skills needed to negotiate life were never taught, built, encouraged, or developed. You have probably been in meetings where someone was so afraid of a boss they could not speak their opinion, or so angry with authority that everything was combative and oppositional.

Psychology works hard on these issues. Getting people to not "lose their power" to other adults and "people-please." Getting out of the inferiority complex that many people feel to other adults with whom they should feel equal, no matter what external status they might possess, is what is needed. Unfortunately, they bow down to them or do the opposite and try to overcompensate by having others bow down to them (the lady on the airplane's boyfriend, or some bosses you might have had might have tried to dominate you into powerlessness like a compliant child).

Therapeutic systems have shown over and over the symptom picture of this developmental arrest and its resolutions. From psychodynamic restructuring of the superego (the parent in the head), to cognitive behavioral therapy's neutralization of the "critical parent thinking," to mindfulness's disengagement and observation of negative voices in order to render them less powerful, and on and on, this is a main clinical emphasis in many systems, and for good reason. Depression from being and feeling one-down in life, or inferior to everyone else, is a real thing. Anxiety from fearing judgment is a real thing. Overcoming the feeling of never measuring up and being out of control is a real thing that can cause pessimism and learned helplessness, as one does not feel like they have control and authority over their own life, etc. Relationships suffer, as does performance.

Clinical symptoms abound from needing sometimes to overcome the "parent" in one's head. As Barack Obama said, "Someone once said that every man is trying to either live up to his father's expectations or make up for his father's mistakes."[1] While that is somewhat oversimplified, as it is not always about fathers, the statement has a lot of truth in it as well. Our parents matter, and when it does not go well, feeling one-down in the world to the detriment of never feeling like an adult is a big deal, and psychology focuses on it a lot.

Surprisingly, I was amazed at how clearly and pervasively the Bible addressed this issue over and over and focused on its remedies. Jesus called on adults to stop trying to please their parents and instead to grow up and please God instead. He said to stop trying to live up to the made-up rules of religious authorities and decide, like an adult, to follow the real teachings of God through your own choices. He said to not bow to religious authorities and treat them as if they are "above" you in some way, teaching that we are all equal. "But you are not to be called 'Rabbi,' for you have one Teacher, and you are all brothers" (Matthew 23:8). Said another way, stop giving away your adult authority to humans, as you are all equal under God. (God has no grandchildren, meaning there is no parent in between an adult and his or her real parent, God.)

And then, as a profound and very productive result, when we do not give away our equality to someone, we can appropriately submit to real authority of a role, instead of the person. When a boss says do something, we can obey without feeling like we have an angry beef with the person or are not equal as a human. We are the adult who signed up to do what that boss said, and if we do not like it, we can find another job. Proper submission to authority is a choice an adult makes, unless you live in an oppressed communist country (or company ☺). It is not personal, and the mature person does not make it personal, unless they psychologically feel one-down inside, and then they have a beef with all authority figures. They can't stand to be told what to do, and that is a characterological problem that usually results in a lot of broken relationships and careers, and, at times, a criminal record. When spouses feel like equals, relationships work well, but if one tries to be the parent, the other one usually won't be happy. And if they say they are . . . are they really? Their friends usually think something is weird.

The scriptures talk about this throughout, railing on humans who try to exert controlling, oppressive parental authority over others. It supports roles of authority, such as employers or the law, but it does not support one human thinking they are somehow "above" others. We are all equal under the law. I love the way Galatians puts it: when we were children, we were under guardians and managers "until the date set by the father." There later developed a bar mitzvah process to celebrate the day you are pronounced to be an adult. It is your life under your management. You can decide things for yourselves in your faith and, soon, your life.

From prescriptions to help us overcome the critical conscience that might have been inherited that is more limiting than God is, to judgment and guilt inside oneself, to condemning lording over one another, to retaining your freedom to not do what other people expect you to do and choosing your own values which might disagree with theirs, to owning and claiming your adult sexual freedom within God's values (not allowed for children, but granted only to adults), to no longer having to obey a parent if you make other choices for yourself and your life, to leaving your family of origin's governing your life and "leaving and cleaving" to establish a new generation of your own household and its government, and on and on, to figuring out your own talents and charting your own course no matter what your parents might choose for you instead, the Bible sounds like a PhD in clinical psychology on this issue. Again, I could not tell sometimes when I read the Bible whether or not I was studying the Bible or I was in one of my clinical trainings.

I could go on and on and list so many other issues, but we don't have the space. But just the four I mentioned above could keep a therapist busy for an entire career. And they do.

The point in listing them is that as psychology addresses all of the issues that cause our mental health problems, including genes, the Bible not only validates them, but is validated by them. And not only the existence of the problems and what causes them, but the big one that convinced me: the prescriptions for healing them. You can in a very literal way say that the Bible's treatment protocols are "evidence based," which is the buzzword today for clinical efficacy. Here are just some of the processes addressed in the Bible that psychology aligns with in the same ways:

- Attachment issues and their resolution
- Being wired for relationship and resolving relational brokenness
- Freedom and self-control as a primary need
- Emotional and behavioral regulation of negative states
- Forgiveness and reconciliation required for ongoing relational success
- Adult maturity as the required equipment for a fruitful life
- Amygdala hijacking and its resolution
- Trauma and grief healing ingredients
- Drive neutralization of the aggressive drive and the love drive working together, so that anger is not destructive, and love is not enabling
- Differentiation of personal boundaries from others, family, and other systems
- Grandiosity, narcissism, arrogance, and pride
- Finding, owning, and developing strengths and talents to fruitfulness
- Skills development for life thriving
- Purposeful living for life thriving
- Thinking paradigms and thinking skills that are healthy
- Safety and trust in relationships
- A purposeful life that produces happiness and thriving
- Altruism and giving
- Limit setting and containment of abuse and toxic behavior

- Goal orientation and a clear path for the science of goal achievement
- Anxiety management and resolution
- Meaning in life
- Life stage development with appropriate tasks for each
- Marriage and parenting skills and development
- Addiction recovery essentials
- Performance anxiety and other performance issues

HOW HEALING AND GROWTH TAKE PLACE THROUGH OPEN-SYSTEM CHANGE

I remember where I was as a graduate student, on the sixth tee at one of my favorite golf courses, when a thought hit me. *Wait . . . Psychology began with Freud, who came from physics and biology, which taught about hydraulics. "Push down here and the water shoots out from over there." Repress an emotion, and it squirts out as a symptom somewhere else. Simple, yet profound.* It changed a lot, as psychology began to look at buried emotions and trauma as the cause of symptoms. So, I asked myself, *What else does physics teach that has to do with psychological processes?*

Thermodynamics . . . OMG! A closed system gets worse over time, and the only way to reverse that is to open the system and infuse the two ingredients of energy and intelligence from the outside to make the energy useful. That is psychological development and healing in a nutshell!

It hit me hard.

That might not sound profound to you, but it was all I could think about for a few years or so. How physics informs human psychological functioning. The human psyche can be a closed system. And it gets worse if it remains a closed system. But if it opens up to two outside ingredients, new energy and new intelligence to utilize that energy, as physics teaches, the psyche grows.

And a wounded or disorganized psyche can heal. That is how both human growth and therapy work . . . from the infant opening up to the energy and love of a connection and the parental intelligence to order that love in useful ways, and good therapy in the same way.

All of the psychological research ever done in meta-analyses of therapies has one finding over all others: it is the therapeutic relationship that heals. And that relationship has to be a supportive energy with warmth (love) and intelligence (truth and guiding principles, wisdom, knowledge, insight, and structure). If those two ingredients, love and truth, are present in the right way, people can heal. (Also, healthy kids come from one kind of environment: high warmth and appropriately high expectations . . . same two ingredients: love and truth-based limits.)

I began to be able to evaluate therapies and systems of therapies by dissecting those ingredients and finding what was helpful and what was not, what dosages were needed by whom and when, with which activities, titrating structure versus process, and other factors. It began to make sense why so many various therapeutic modalities were all able to show some effectiveness, depending on how those ingredients were present or not and to what degree. Physics really helped me in developing a metapsychology of treatment, and later, John Townsend and I together developed that construct further to use in designing our treatment programs in the hospitals that produced the results I talked about earlier.

But, in terms of my faith, it was like a light switch going on. It explained the whole message of the Bible about human existence:

1. We were created to be connected to energy (God) and intelligence (God).
2. We separated from him and became our individual "closed systems" without the energy from the relationship with

God and His love, and without His "ways" living in us, his truth, ordering our existence. On our own, as a closed system separated from Him, the human race has not done well since the Fall of Creation.

3. Entropy had its way and humanity got worse as we remained separated from Love and helpful input of Intelligence beyond ourselves. As the Bible says, we are "lost," and that means separated from Life.
4. Then, God entered the system, human life, Himself to bring us back to number one above. He invites us to get reconnected to Him and each other and be loved and guided back to restoration. He brought to us those two ingredients all over again.

That is the gospel in a nutshell. Jesus to enter into our closed system, bringing life.

From there, I could see how everything the Bible talks about is the reversal of the brokenness of relationship with God and others, and with ourselves, along with the structuring of life in learning better ways: His ways. The Designer's ways. (Do not rescue an angry man, for example.) He was and is reversing entropy, death, in all of life as He enters in and offers us a relationship with infinite Love and infinite Truth. The two factors I saw in physics: energy and intelligence. He empowers us, and He instructs us.

I won't belabor this further . . . it is a whole other book. But suffice it to say it is another example of how everything I learned in the science of psychology pointed me back to what God had said and Jesus had done.

When I reconnected to Him, I found a Source of energy and love and support that I needed, and His ways healed me and set me on a different path of growth. He invaded my "closed system." Who knew that Freud and the Bible actually agree on some things . . . atheist that he was. Side note observation . . . it is funny to watch so many modern day popularists trash Freud. Of course, much of what he said has been reformulated and morphed in many ways.

He was not right about everything. But he did open the conversation on much good, such as that personality has structure to it and is developed in stages, dreams mean something, emotions need processing, relationships are formative, how the process of grief and bereavement affect clinical issues, we are symbolic creatures, we repeat internalized relationships and act them out in present relationships, we are destined to repeat conflictual patterns until they are rewired, cognitive restructuring is important, growth is a process, etc. Many of the propositions of "new" therapies are not new at all. Most of the "trashers" I find have never read original sources but just repeat something about Freud they read in a newspaper or some professor told them. I am not a Freudian in the classic sense of the term. But I can appreciate what his integration of the physical (biology) and physics (laws) gave rise to.

Seeing life as a closed system until we open the system to God explained much about theology and the Bible. It still does. The number one tenet of the entire Bible, and especially the New Testament is one word: connection to God. Jesus called it abiding:

> ***Abide in Me, and I in you. As the branch cannot bear fruit of itself, unless it abides in the vine, neither can you, unless you abide in Me.*** (John 15:4 NKJV)

All fruitfulness in life depends on a connected relationship, including humans. But the Source and the number one relationship we need is to be connected to Him. That is what started the whole process for me in that dorm room. Matthew 6:33 said to seek the kingdom of God (a relationship with Him) and His righteousness (His intelligence and truth) and all these things shall be added unto you. I have learned that to be true. And when a person does that, he or she finds that He immediately tells them to get connected to others, and the healing can begin.

HEALTHY INTEGRATION BETWEEN THE TWO DRIVES THAT MAKE US HUMAN: LOVE AND AGGRESSION

Okay, you might want to skip this one as it is a bit esoteric but was powerful to me in how psychology validated the Bible, so here we go.

Basically, humans, at our deepest core, have two strong drives. There are others, but these are primary. The first is the drive to connect, the relational drive, and the second is the drive to assert, the aggressive drive. The connection drive is one of love, and the aggressive drive is one that moves to make things the way we feel they ought to be and what we want to be. For example, even an infant screams and pushes against what is not the way they feel it ought to be. Later, that same drive builds houses or careers.

In the beginning, these are very separate and divided. Soothe the infant with love, and you see little aggression. But frustrate the infant, and you see the aggressive drive come running to the rescue in absolute rage. Immature adult humans still have love and aggression split (think borderline personalities). Good and bad is the way they experience life. *Love me, and we are fine. Deprive me, and I will rage at you. I will fix this and you too!*

As we mature, we are able to bring those drives together, and they neutralize each other. They utilize the good aspects of each other and mitigate the destructiveness of the split. For example, immature love is idealized, like with a narcissistic or borderline personality disorder when they instantly fall in love and the other person is wonderful, luring them into a drug trip of overwhelming positive feeling states. It is all love, all the time. All good. But frustrate them in some way, and you do not get a loving piece of feedback when they are angry. Instead, you get rage, and attack. They see you as horrible and will rage at you and attack you, and even try to bring you down. All aggression, no love. There is no "gray"; it is all black and white. This is immature personality organization.

Also, immature love has no truth, an aggressive function, active in it. It is split and loves without enforcing limits. It becomes enabling and idealizing. As the drives cannot work together, the enabler just loves without ever pushing back in any way as long as it just stays in its "loving" mode. Codependency reigns . . . until one day they might have had enough and file for divorce. Watch the aggressive drive sometimes kick in during those battles in the immature one! It can get ugly.

Many women will tell you that in the beginning, the narcissist loved them obsessively and did everything for them. Until he got disappointed in some say, like she said no to something. Then, it flips. He goes on the attack and love is out the window.

After infancy, as maturity grows through a loving parent who is integrated and loves the child with limits, increasing maturity processes bring these drives together and develop an increasing ability in the child to love the parent even when the parent sometimes frustrates them. Over and over, the rageful child is soothed and yet over time and increasingly, gradually put back to bed and *not* allowed to, once again, as a toddler, ragefully get the parent to come rescue them and sleep in the parent's room just to placate. The parent puts loving limits on the child and does not wrongfully become the perceived "all good" parent, doing whatever the child wants, instead of being a loving and at times, frustrating parent.

For example, raging toddlers are lovingly given limits and required to be in time-out until they stop screaming and can agree to be nice. I fondly remember telling our oldest, Olivia, at times when I put her in time-out: "I'll listen when you stop screaming and use your words." Or "Be quiet until that little timer goes off, and then you can get out." In that way, the drives begin to integrate, and they can be angry or sad at something without the rage and learn to accept the word "no" without hating someone, as the woman on the airplane's boyfriend did. (Boyfriends who act like toddlers sometimes need a good time-out. I remember a song we taught our kids to sing: "You get what you get, and you don't get upset." It was time for them to not attack the word "no" like it was some kind of enemy, and learn to accept it.)

With time and many experiences, children's drives become neutralized through a neutralized parent who had firm limits along with love, instead of no limits or only angry limits with no love. (This is why anger is one of the worst parenting tools that parents try to use, as well as overindulging children, on the other side.) What does this integrated parenting produce? A healthy psyche that can have a long-term relationship with an imperfect person, among other qualities. The ability to love a person even when they sometimes frustrate you. When they have a conflict, they can be angry, but in their anger, not sin, as the Bible puts it (Ephesians 4:26). They lovingly confront their spouse and they work it out . . . provided the spouse can also hear the frustration of being confronted and lovingly respond in kind. That is an integrated personality. It leads to a whole host of psychological maturation and abilities, such as impulse control and emotional regulation. Mature people do not act out or let their emotional states overcome them. Again, think of the impulsivity of borderline personalities among whom splitting is a key feature.

And here is the point that amazed me. When I learned this concept and saw how critical it was to all of life, relationships, and maturity, the Bible screamed something out at me.

The entirety of the Scriptures speak of a God who is integrated in love and aggression.

> ***[In Him,] Love and faithfulness meet together; righteousness and peace kiss each other.*** (Psalm 85:10)
>
> ***The Word became flesh and made his dwelling among us. We have seen his glory, the glory of the one and only Son, who came from the Father, full of grace and truth.*** (John 1:14)

God is constantly referred to as a Person of grace and truth, mercy and righteousness, and other integrated descriptions of these two qualities.

God is a Person whose "love and limits" come together, integrated. Jesus confronts the adulterer, but does it in love: "Neither do I condemn you; go and sin no more" (John 8:11 NKJV). Sounds like a good parent speaking to a child in time-out. No anger, but clear, loving limits. Love and limits at the same time.

The entire gospel is a presentation of Someone who is calling us to develop into the same maturity. It calls us to learn to stop raging and condemning when someone fails us, or the opposite—loving them without rules or expectations or structure. When someone frustrates you, speak the truth in love (see Ephesians 4:15). Love *while* you set your limits. Do both together.

Remember what I said about drive regulation and impulse control? It is an integrated life that he calls us to, and the more we get integrated, the better self-control we have and the better our relationships are as well. Goals are reached as we can internally say no to pleasure seeking, frustrating our impulsive child inside with a clear no, when we should be doing more sales calls that day instead of going out and seeking fun. Delay of gratification is increased. Conflicts are resolved instead of further disintegrating into broken relationships. Parenting skills grow. Just a fruit of a life that has learned to "speak the truth in love." Your internal limits, saying no to yourself, will work way better if that voice is kind.

This is an amazing gospel in my view . . . amazing. And learning how drive neutralization works, letting love and limits, love and aggression, empathy and confrontation, being both relational and task oriented, all work together, opened up the Bible to me in a whole new way.

I could go on and on about psychology and the Bible . . . it has been my life's work. Where do multiple personalities come from? From being created in the image of God, who has many, many different parts to Him, but He never splits. Trauma from living in a fallen world splits a victim, and the parts take on their own lives. Why is the New Testament so against guilt? Why does it offer us no condemnation, even when we fail? Same reason that psychologists have discovered that guilt is crippling and never leads to maturity. Only real sorrow, remorse that is focused on the other person and how I hurt them and myself, effects change. Something the Bible calls "godly sorrow" (2 Corinthians 7:10 NKJV).

I could continue with so many other concepts of psychology that are inherent in the Scriptures, but I just wanted you to know one thing: this is one science that validates the truth of the Bible for me.

Conclusion and an Invitation to You

If you remember from the preface, this book began as a desire to talk to my friends about God . . . and help them understand how I could be "one of *those*?" How I could be one of those people who actually believes in the "true-true" version of who Jesus is? From that initial desire, I decided to treat it like a real book and share it with a broader audience. And to write it in a way that others who are believers who want to share their faith with their friends could pass it on and begin their own conversations. Hopefully, it has been helpful to both groups.

So, now you know how I came to find faith from my own deep need for God to show up and help me when I needed Him most, then experienced His reality in many different ways, and after that, had to find answers for many intellectual and personal obstacles that I had. Thanks for going through that journey with me. And I have to say, at this point in the writing, it has been a very meaningful experience for me to recall how faithful and dependable He has been for so many years now. Recalling and remembering are good things.

In one sense, I could have written a lot more . . . there are so many other questions I have grappled with and didn't have space to cover, and so many experiences I have had that I would love to share as well. Maybe another book! ☺

As we close, I want to extend an invitation . . . to whoever personally wants to take that next step. It may be that same step that I took that day in my dorm room that took faith to a deeper level, or it could be a *first* step for you in this whole arena. For others, it could be a reboot of faith, as their own path has taken them in some different directions.

The best way that I know to do that is directly from the Bible and the words of Jesus. He said it this way:

> ***Behold, I stand at the door and knock. If anyone hears My voice and opens the door, I will come in to him and dine with him, and he with Me.*** (Revelation 3:20 NKJV)

Faith in Jesus is not primarily a collection of "beliefs" or a philosophy. It is a *relationship*. It is the relationship that God created you for in the very beginning of why He made you. He created you to love you, and share love, life, and purpose with you. In fact, as I have told many, you can begin by just sincerely asking Him "Are you real? If so, show me. I am open to knowing."

But even though we were all created to have a relationship with Him, as the story of the Bible reveals, for all of us, we all have breached that relationship in various ways. We either have ignored Him, have rejected Him, or have strayed in some way. At the very least, we all have violated the first commandment, "have no other gods before me" (Exodus 20:3), as well as many other commandments. When we run our own lives apart from Him, like I did, by definition, we are our own god, instead of Him.

But he wants us! The Bible says "he jealously longs for the spirit he has caused to dwell in us" (James 4:5). He wants us back in the relationship that was lost with Him. Just like when you have been betrayed in one of your personal relationships, reconciling it takes forgiveness. The one who betrayed you has to do something simple: own what they did, and ask for your forgiveness. Then, when you forgive them, they can receive it from you and the two of you can start anew. Together again.

This is the message of the Gospel of Jesus. He comes to us, invites us to just admit we have turned against God and failed His perfect standard in various ways, and simply receive the forgiveness He is offering, thereby having our relationship reconciled. We can begin anew.

The "good news" is that we get a clean slate. No judgment or condemnation awaits. As Jesus said, He did not come to condemn or judge the world, but to seek and to save that which was lost (see John 3:17). We are totally accepted when we come to Him, like I told my friend on his deathbed in a previous chapter. When he received the Passover Lamb of Jesus, it paid for all of his "sins," a word we have grown allergic to in modern times. What it literally means is we have "missed the target" or have a "fault." Just like an archer misses the bull's eye, we have missed it in life in different ways. In some ways more than others, and some people more than others, but all of us to some degree match this definition of "sin." Moral failures, relationship failures, and even ways we are at "fault" before God. We have hurt people and done things that do not give life either to ourselves or to people we care about. In God's court of law, we are all guilty. It is a hard word for us to stomach because it often carries so much judgment and guilt when used poorly, but its truth still remains for all of us in some way or another. You are not Hitler, but we all have failed in some way.

But the good news is that the Judge himself says He will pay our fine for us. That is what the death of Christ was about. He "paid" for our transgressions, our sins, our ways that actually deserve judgment. When we accept Him, then we are forgiven.

All it requires, like reconciling any relationship, is receiving that forgiveness. And like in any relationship, when we truly are sorry, we say "I'm sorry . . . and I want to do better by you." That second step is called repentance. We get forgiven for the past, and desire to do better for Him and others in the future. That is what it means to call him Lord. We agree to answer to Him and not just ourselves. Then we experience what Paul said to the people of Rome:

> ***That is, the message concerning faith that we proclaim: If you declare with your mouth, "Jesus is Lord," and believe in your heart that God raised him from the dead, you will be saved. For it is with your heart that you believe and are justified, and it is with your mouth that you profess your faith and are saved.*** (Romans 10:8–10)

It sounds simple and hard to believe for many . . . but it is a free gift. We will never be "good enough," and that is what forgiveness and grace are all about. God is the only one who could be perfect enough to stand in our place at the Judge's bench.

And there is better news . . . He knows we won't do it perfectly in the future, either. We will make mistakes along the way. He promises to continue to forgive and, past that, to help us grow and get better. Can an addict promise to be perfect forever from day one? No . . . but they can promise to head in that direction and ask for His help. And if they do fail, ask and realize His forgiveness and begin another day. As the Bible says, His mercies "are new every morning" (Lamentations 3:23). Just like a good parent, He will be with you as you learn and grow, and help you continue to turn into the best person you were designed to be.

He also doesn't want you to do this alone. He says that once you come "home" to being back with your Heavenly Father, you will need some good "brothers and sisters" to live it all out with, in relationship together. So, find a good group of people (a church) who are on that path with you, and who can help you. (Don't let that word "church" scare you . . . there really are some good ones out there. ☺)

And I would strongly suggest beginning by reading the gospel of John. You will find it in the New Testament, the fourth book. It contains the most famous verse 16: "For God so loved the world that He gave his one and only Son, that whoever believes in Him shall not perish but have eternal life." If you open the door of your heart, like He referred to in the verse above from Revelation, He will come into your heart and life, and your relationship will begin. Just like the rest of John chapter 3 says, just like the wind . . . you won't see Him but you will begin to see His movements in your heart and life.

As C. S. Lewis was quoted earlier, this is a decision about "true-true." It is not an option among other equally valid options. Jesus made a claim that no one else makes. He said that He is "*the* Way," and the "*only* Way." That is hard to swallow for many. But He specifically said this: "I am the way and the truth and the life. No one comes to the Father except through me" (John 14:6). Not popular to some, as they see it as too "exclusive" . . . but it is what He said. But that makes sense to me . . . if there is only one God, One Creator, we have to deal with Him directly. We never get into a person's house by thinking someone else across town can invite us to that person's home. Instead, we have to deal with the real owner of it all. And He won't refuse you, as He said many times. That is why it is *not* exclusive at all. He invites every single person in His own way.

I will close with the summary of it all that the apostle Paul gave in the Areopagus of Greece. Remember Paul? He was the Jewish leader who was killing Christians, thinking they were all wrong. And then Jesus appeared to him on the Damascus Road, and Paul was converted to faith in Jesus. This man who was fighting Christians realized through a direct visitation that Jesus was the real God, and then did a total 180, spending the rest of his life spreading the gospel, being beaten, imprisoned, and tortured as he did. Ultimately he died for preaching what he knew was "true-true."

Here is what he said on Mars Hill:

> *Now all the Athenians and foreigners who lived there spent their time doing nothing more than hearing and articulating new ideas.*
>
> *Then Paul stood up in the meeting of the Areopagus and said, "Men of Athens, I see that in every way you are very religious. For as I walked around and examined your objects of worship, I even found an altar with this inscription:*
>
> *TO AN UNKNOWN GOD.*
>
> *"Therefore, what you worship as something unknown, I now proclaim to you.*
>
> *"The God who made the world and everything in it is the Lord of heaven and earth and does not live in temples made by human hands. Nor is He served by human hands, as if He needed anything, because He Himself gives everyone life and breath and everything else. From one man He made every nation of men, that they should inhabit the whole earth; and*

He determined their appointed times and the boundaries of their lands.

"God intended that they would seek Him and perhaps reach out for Him and find Him, though He is not far from each one of us. 'For in Him we live and move and have our being.' As some of your own poets have said, 'We are His offspring.' Therefore, being offspring of God, we should not think that the Divine Being is like gold or silver or stone, an image formed by man's skill and imagination.

"Although God overlooked the ignorance of earlier times, He now commands all people everywhere to repent. For He has set a day when He will judge the world with justice by the Man He has appointed. He has given proof of this to everyone by raising Him from the dead."

When they heard about the resurrection of the dead, some began to mock him, but others said, "We want to hear you again on this topic." At that, Paul left the Areopagus. But some joined him and believed, including Dionysius the Areopagite, a woman named Damaris, and others who were with them. (Acts 17:21–34 BSB)

So, that is what I would like to pass on to you . . . that invitation. I hope you try Him and see for yourself. He promised that if anyone seeks Him with their whole heart, they will find Him. Open the door, and watch. He will begin to reveal Himself if you truly want to know Him.

I hope you do. And thanks for listening.

Henry Cloud
Nashville, Tennessee
2024

Acknowledgments

There are too many great people to even name who nurtured, guided, and nourished my path to God and journey with Him over many years. But here are a few that I wanted to mention, some of whom have passed on from this life, and I am sure that I have failed to remember some who really helped along the way. If you were there and I did not name you, please know that you are appreciated. Thanks:

To Mama and Daddy . . . for starting me out and seeing a real faith expressed in giving to so many others.

To Twick Morrison, who is now in heaven. You were my earliest teacher.

To the counselors at Camp Rockmont way back when . . . you don't remember this kid, but you helped me. And to other youth workers who poured their time into us when kids like me were still years away from consciousness.

To Bill Bright, who is now in heaven. What you started in Cru had significant impact on me. And along with Cru, Josh McDowell, who provided many answers to questions, Mary Graham, and the folks at the Jesus Film Project in its early days. And Steve Sellers, who worked alongside me to communicate spiritual growth and resolving emotional problems are addressed as one.

To Danny Carrol, Darrel Boch, Probe Ministries, and Scott Rae for your help in my SMU years.

To Bill and Julie Jemison . . . you are mentioned throughout this story, and without you, I am not sure there would even be one.

To Dr. Edward Atkinson, also now in heaven . . . my best pal then who made the first phone call that led me out of the desert and walked me through some tough days. And to Bob Loeb, my other frat bro who kept me connected to God when I wasn't really "both feet in." You were truly inspirational.

To those whose writings and/or relationship in the very early days as I began my road to God that laid a foundation for me . . . Hal Lindsay, Francis Schaffer, Thomas Merton, the Desert Fathers, David Wilkerson, J. I. Packer, Adrian Rogers, John Wimber, Jack Hayford, Charles Ryrie, Dallas Theological Seminary, John Wesley, Charles Spurgeon, Jonathan Edwards, Scott Peck, Hannah Whitall Smith, Brother Andrew, Dr. Otto Kernberg, Martin Buber, Soren Kierkegaard . . . and many more.

From your classrooms and direct hands-on mentorship . . . Dr. Bruce Narramore, Dr. Frank Minirth, Phil Sutherland, Dr. John Carter.

For offering me a home and family for the not-so-adult me to finish growing up, Guy and Christi Owen.

For being the best traveling companion one could ever have over the years and growing together through many stages of faith, Dr. John Townsend.

For being my pastor and friend, Ger Jones.

For showing me a lot about God's character being His healing agent and mentor to me, Dr. Althea Horner.

To many of my clients that I am not at liberty to name, but who have been great models to me, and from whom I learned a lot about the life of faith, commitment, character, and more . . . I am forever indebted to you. Even the "difficult" ones . . . you helped me grow. ☺

To my friends and colleagues for all the great years we worked together at Willow Creek and the Global Leadership Summit.

To those who have used their prophetic gifts to speak into my life at very important moments, you know who you are. I thank you for your courage and using your gifts well, which at times were God's voice to me and at key points altered the direction of my life and work.

To three people who live a life of miracles and who have modeled the belief and reality that God still works, more recently to me, Dr. Randy Clark, Dr. Heidi Baker, Joanne Moody. I will never forget your healing prayers for me when I was in so much physical pain.

To John Lang . . . for prodding me to finally begin writing this book, and for your modeling faith and perseverance through a season of horrible tragedy, coming out on the other side with even deeper faith and testimony of a life well lived.

To Tori . . . my spiritual confidant and partner in life for showing me the love and character of Jesus, every single day. You are his "hands and feet" to so many people. The best gift He ever gave me.

To Olivia and Lucy . . . for expanding my heart and showing me what it is like to be a father . . . giving me a peek into the joy that the Bible speaks of when it shares what God feels for His kids. I know His love for us is infinitely more love than I have for you because of who He is, but I can't imagine how it could be . . . even though I know it is true. You have brought me closer to Him in a million ways.

To Shannon Miser-Marven, my agent . . . for believing in this book and stewarding it as only you can. You rock. And to Jan Miller, for founding Dupree-Miller and all you have done to steward my work for the last twenty years.

And to Sealy Yates for overseeing so many of my books integrating faith and life. You were key in the early work of figuring it all out.

To Daisy Hutton, for having faith in this book and agreeing to not only publish it but edit it with love and care. Thanks for putting up with my goofy "voice" and resisting the editorial impulse to make it sound better than it actually is.

To some of my favorite "seeker skeptics" who push back in the best ways. You have helped me with this book immensely, and I love our friendly "debates." Thank you for being there in this process and in my life: Lexi, Greg, and Alby.

To Jayson Teagle for helping me think through working with churches to fight the mental health crisis. Your passion for the mission is inspiring.

To my weekly group of fellow travelers who were God's family to me for so long: Terry and Monsita, Jeanne and Bill, Tori Cloud.

To the best four-legged companions, who beyond a doubt showed me God's creative genius. No one but the Ultimate Designer could have made German Shepherds and Dobermans: Bonnie, Greta, Handi (bless your heart), Riley, and Finley. You made me really research the Bible and find proof that dogs will be in heaven!

To some special friends who have been a very meaningful community to me over the years as we have walked through life, figuring out parenting, marriage, and fun. I consider it to have been a real gift of God's love to have given you guys to me, Tori, and our family, and part of my spiritual path: Daniel and Pamela Salzman, Cooper and Hayes Jackson, Sarah and Jon Aibel, Roy Newman and Nicole Johnson.

To the entire Ochs clan for modeling a family committed to faith and life. You have made me better.

To all of you and others,

Thank you.

Notes

PART II: A HELPING HAND

1 Sigmund Freud, *Dora: An Analysis of a Case of Hysteria* (Collier, 1963 [1905]).

CHAPTER 6: THE TRUTH IS TRUE

1 C. S. Lewis, *Mere Christianity* (Collins, 1952), 54–56.

CHAPTER 8: SCIENCE AS AN OBSTACLE TO FAITH

1 Josh McDowell, *More Than a Carpenter* (Tyndale, 1977).

2 "The Anthropic Principle," *Horizon*, season 23, episode 18, May 18, 1987, BBC. Available at https://www.dailymotion.com/video/x615j43.

3 "The Anthropic Principle."

4 "The Anthropic Principle."

5 John Horgan, "Remembering Big Bang Basher Fred Hoyle," *Scientific American*, April 7, 2020, https://blogs.scientificamerican.com/cross-check/remembering-big-bang-basher-fred-hoyle.

6 A. L. Van Den Herik, *The Shortest Leap: The Rational Underpinnings of Faith in Jesus*, Kindle Edition (WestBow Press, 2020), citing Hugh Ross, *The Creator and the Cosmos*, 3rd ed. (NavPress, 2001).

7 Van Den Herik, *The Shortest Leap*, citing Ross, *The Creator and the Cosmos.*

8 Arno Penzias, "Creation Is Supported by All the Data So Far," in *Cosmos, Bios, Theos: Scientists Reflect on Science, God, and the Origins of the Universe, Life, and* Homo Sapiens, edited by Henry Margenau and Roy Abraham Varghese (Open Court, 1992), 83.

9 Charles Darwin, letter to Asa Gray, February 8 or 9, 1860, https://www.darwinproject.ac.uk/letter/?docId=letters/DCP-LETT-2701.xml.

10 "Einstein Believes in 'Spinoza's God,'" *New York Times*, April 25, 1929, https://timesmachine.nytimes.com/timesmachine/1929/04/25/95932842.html?pageNumber=30.

CHAPTER 9: CAN I TRUST THE BIBLE?

1 "William F. Albright: Toward a More Conservative View," *Christianity Today*, January 18, 1963, p. 3.

2 Josh McDowell, *More Than a Carpenter* (Tyndale, 1977), 44.

3 McDowell, *More Than a Carpenter*, 44.

4 W. F. Albright, *From the Stone Age to Christianity* (Johns Hopkins Press, 1957), 387.

5 Albright, *From the Stone Age to Christianity.*

6 McDowell, *More Than a Carpenter.*

7 Daniel B. Wallace, personal correspondence with Josh McDowell, January 6, 2003, cited in Josh McDowell and Sean McDowell, *More Than a Carpenter*, revised and updated ed. (Tyndale, 2009).

8 Frederic Kenyon, *The Bible and Archaeology* (Harper and Row, 1940), 288–289.

CHAPTER 11: THE GREATEST OBSTACLE OF ALL

1 Karen E. Adolph et al., "How Do You Learn to Walk? Thousands of Steps and Dozens of Falls Per Day," *Psychological Science* 23, no. 11 (2012): 1387–1394, https://www.ncbi.nlm.nih.gov/pmc/articles/PMC3591461.

CHAPTER 12: PSYCHOLOGY AND FAITH

1 Barack Obama, *The Audacity of Hope: Thoughts on Reclaiming the American Dream* (Crown, 2006).

About the Author

Dr. Henry Cloud is an acclaimed leadership expert, clinical psychologist, and *New York Times* bestselling author. His forty-five books, including the iconic *Boundaries*, have sold nearly 20 million copies worldwide. In addition to decades of clinical work, he has an extensive executive coaching background and experience as a leadership consultant, now devoting the majority of his time to working with CEOs, leadership teams, and executives to improve performance, leadership skills, and culture.